The
Twilight
of the Old
Unionism

ISSUES IN WORK AND HUMAN RESOURCES

Daniel J.B. Mitchell, Series Editor

BEYOND UNIONS AND COLLECTIVE BARGAINING
Leo Troy

CYBERUNION
Empowering Labor Through Computer Technology
Arthur B. Shostak

WORKING IN THE TWENTY-FIRST CENTURY
Policies for Economic Growth Through Training, Opportunity, and Education
David I. Levine

INCOME INEQUALITY IN AMERICA
An Analysis of Trends
Paul Ryscavage

HARD LABOR
Poor Women and Work in the Post-Welfare Era
Joel F. Handler and Lucie White, editors

NONUNION EMPLOYEE REPRESENTATION
History, Contemporary Practice, and Policy
Bruce E. Kaufman and Daphne Gottlieb Taras, editors

LABOR REGULATION IN A GLOBAL ECONOMY
George Tsogas

FAMILY LEAVE POLICY
The Political Economy of Work and Family in America
Steven K. Wisensale

COLLECTIVE BARGAINING IN THE PUBLIC SECTOR
The Experience of Eight States
Joyce M. Najita and James L. Stern, editors

PAYING FOR PERFORMANCE
An International Comparison
Michelle Brown and John S. Heywood, editors

THE FUTURE OF PRIVATE SECTOR UNIONISM IN THE UNITED STATES
James T. Bennett and Bruce E. Kaufman, editors

THE CYBERUNION HANDBOOK
Transforming Labor Through Computer Technology
Arthur B. Shostak, editor

CHILD LABOR
An American History
Hugh D. Hindman

INDUSTRIAL RELATIONS TO HUMAN RESOURCES AND BEYOND
The Evolving Process of Employee Relations Management
Bruce E. Kaufman, Richard A. Beaumont, and Roy B. Helfgott, editors

EMPLOYMENT EQUITY AND AFFIRMATIVE ACTION
An International Comparison
Harish C. Jain, Peter J. Sloan, and Frank M. Horwitz
with Simon Taggar and Nan Weiner

WORKING IN SILICON VALLEY
Economic and Legal Analysis of High-Velocity Labor Market
Alan Hyde

The Twilight of the Old Unionism

Leo Troy

M.E. Sharpe
Armonk, New York
London, England

Library of Congress Cataloging-in-Publication Data

Troy, Leo
    The twilight of the Old Unionism / Leo Troy
      p. cm. — (Issues in work and human resources)
    Includes bibliographical references and index
    ISBN 0-7656-0746-8 (alk. paper)
      1. Labor unions—United States—History. 2. Labor movement—United States—
History. I. Title. II. Series.

HD6508.T745 2004
331.88′0973—dc22

                                                    2003061432

Printed in the United States of America

The paper used in this publication meets the minimum requirements of
American National Standard for Information Sciences
Permanence of Paper for Printed Library Materials,
ANSI Z 39.48-1984.

MK

BM (c)   10   9   8   7   6   5   4   3   2   1

TABLE OF CONTENTS

LIST OF TABLES

FOREWORD

Leo Troy is one of the top researchers in the field of unionization trends. In this volume, he continues his interpretation of the empirical evidence. In the United States, Troy argues, the union sector is really bifurcated. In private employment, which Troy identifies with "Old Unionism," there is steady erosion of union representation rates. Troy finds that this erosion is largely due to market forces and competition rather than to managerial resistance. In contrast, government employment is identified by Troy with "New Unionism," which shows no signs of eroding. New Unionism, because it is in the public sector, is largely shielded from marketplace competition.

Although some researchers have thought that the United States was relatively unique in exhibiting these trends, Troy finds them also in other countries, notably Canada. Legal institutions may slow down the decline in Old Unionism. And the public sector may be larger in many other countries than it is in the United States. However, the decline of the unionization rate in the private sector is a near-worldwide characteristic.

Old Unionism, Troy proposes, will not die out in the United States but will be confined to limited market niches. The growth in importance of public sector membership, however, changes the demographic character of unions away from the traditional blue collar model and toward white collar workers such as teachers. Moreover, the shrinkage in the private sector is moving unions toward political action and linkage with the Democratic Party.

Troy's findings and conclusions will be controversial for some readers and a confirmation for others. Either way, the findings raise interesting questions. Will what Troy terms "individual representation," that is, the nonunion employment relationship, lead to union substitutes such as legislative workplace regulation and/or employment litigation? Union workers tend to be more likely to receive job-related benefits such as health care and defined-benefit pensions. What will happen to the American system of semi-private social insurance if such benefits erode along with Old Unionism? What happens to the two-party political system in the United States if one party is dependent on a sector that is declining? Regardless of their views, readers will want to consider these issues in light of this volume.

Daniel J.B. Mitchell
Series Editor

PREFACE

This book completes my trilogy on labor relations in the United States. The first, *The New Unionism in the New Society* (1994), addressed the public sector. It analyzed the public sector unionism that arose in the federal, state, and local governments following President Kennedy's Executive Order 10988 of 1962. I referred to this as the New Unionism. Only a few public sector labor organizations had existed before then, and these were mainly in the U.S. Post Office. They could not engage in collective bargaining or in strikes. In fact, the union that is now the largest in the American Labor Movement, the National Education Association, Independent, as well as the American Federation of Teachers, AFL-CIO, both rejected collective bargaining and strikes until the 1960s, as the organizations identified themselves as professional groups, not unions. However, early in the 1960s, both transformed themselves into unions and embraced the strike and collective bargaining. Now these two organizations are the leaders of the New Unionism and will soon become the dominant unions in the American Labor Movement. Two factors—the size of their combined membership, which is well over 3.5 million, and that their members are professionals—justify this forecast.

The Twilight of the Old Unionism details the decline of private sector labor organization, its diminished role in the American Labor Movement, and the reasons for the decline. I call private sector labor organization the Old Unionism because unions originated in the private labor market. My second book on American labor relations, *Beyond Unions and Collective Bargaining* (1999), analyzed nonunion labor relations. The nonunion labor market is the largest part of the labor market. Despite numerous treatises on unions, professional scholars had given no consideration to the nonunion alternative to organized labor relations; for them, only one form of employer–employee relations existed, the organized system. Yet, today, the nonunion labor market accounts for over 87 percent of all wage and salaried employees, and in the private sector alone, it accounts for more than 90 percent of workers. In the second book I dealt with how the terms and conditions of employment are resolved, and argued that self-representation is a viable system of employee relations. To paraphrase a statement, perhaps apocryphal, of Milton Friedman, attempting to gain acceptance of the book was like hitting one's head against the wall.

The *Twilight of the Old Unionism* argues that the Old Unionism is in an irreversible decline: it will not recover either the membership or the market share it had in the recent or historical past. However, *twilight* does not mean the extinction of the Old Unionism. To the contrary, collective bargaining will remain a key factor in determining working conditions in several important industrial sectors, such as automobile manufacturing, construction, and transportation—air, rail, and over the road. Moreover, the Old Unionism still accounts for the majority of union members, is richer than the New Unionism, and is the largest and wealthiest among all G-7 countries. Abroad, public sector unionism dominates the labor movements in membership and market share; but that will soon become the model in the United States as well.

The transformation enhances the role of organized labor in the political life of the United States. Partly for that reason, the book concludes that the Democratic Party has become the de facto Labor Party of the United States. Part of the data I shall present on this subject are derived from my testimony before the U.S. Senate Committee on Rules (April 2000) and the House Subcommittee on Oversight of the Ways and Means Committee (June 2000).

This book consists of two major parts: First, chapters 1, 2, and 3 address what happened to the Old Unionism, why it happened, and why its decline is irreversible. Second, chapters 4, 5, and 6 analyze the consequences of the twilight of the Old Unionism: the emergence of "The Brave New World of the American Labor Movement," the convergence of American and international unionism, and the Democratic Party's becoming the Labor Party of the United States. My conclusions are found in Chapter 7.

ACKNOWLEDGMENTS

I wish to thank the *Journal of Labor Research* and its editor, Professor James T. Bennett, for permission to use articles published by the *Journal*, for which support came from the John M. Olin Institute for Employment and Policy. These articles were: "Twilight for Organized Labor" (*Journal of Labor Research*, Spring 2001), the article for the symposium "The Future of Private Sector Unions in the United States: Part II, 2002"; and "Is the Future of Unionism in Cyber Space?" (*Journal of Labor Research*, Spring 2003).

I also wish to acknowledge the help, both intellectual and material, I received from the Social Philosophy and Policy Center at Bowling Green State University. In particular, I appreciate the discussion at the Center's colloquium in May 2003.

I also thank Mr. Ka-Neng Au, business librarian of the Dana Library, Rutgers University–Newark, for his assiduous and scholarly work. I am grateful to my son, Alexander Troy, for valuable input on Chapter 4.

Finally, I thank Susanna Sharpe for her excellent copyediting and the staff at M.E. Sharpe, Esther L. Clark, Lynn Taylor, and Ana Erlic, for their patience and assistance.

The Twilight of the Old Unionism

1

THE FLOW AND EBB
OF THE OLD UNIONISM

From Trough to Peak, 1933–1953

The argument of this book is that the Old Unionism is in a permanent state of decline.[1] Its statistical record during the twentieth and into the new century, reported in Table 1.1, resembles a ride on the Cyclone, the renowned roller coaster at Coney Island, New York. Analytically, the record of the Old Unionism partly mimics the Kondratieff long-term business cycle.[2] Unlike that cycle for business conditions, I do not foresee an eventual resurgence of the Old Unionism. The "twilight" of the Old Unionism means that it will regain neither its peak levels in membership, about 17 million in 1970, nor its market share, 36 percent in 1953 (Troy and Sheflin 1985). However, "twilight" also means that the Old Unionism will continue to be a decisive factor in the key industries of auto and steel manufacturing, construction, and transportation. The term also means that the Old Unionism will increasingly shift its focus and resources from its trade union functions—organizing and bargaining—and become a major player in the political life of this country. The Old Unionism represents very large financial resources and organizations that receive huge sums in annual income. Together with the wealth and income of the New Unionism, the American Labor Movement[3] owns at least $10 billion in assets and receives up to $14 billion annually in income (Masters and Atkin 1997 on assets; my estimate on income).

The starting point of the Old Unionism's long cycle over the twentieth into the beginning of the twenty-first century is the pit of the Great Depression in 1933.[4] From a trough of 3.5 million in membership and a market share of under 15 percent, it rose to a peak density in 1953 of 36 percent and total membership of about 17 million in 1970. So depressed

Table 1.1

The Old Unionism, 1900–2002

Year	Membership (thousands)	Density (percent)
1900	916	6.5
1933	3,194	15.5
1953	15,540	35.7*
1970	16,978*	29.1
2002	8,652	8.6

Sources: For 1900–1970, Leo Troy and Neil Sheflin, *Union Sourcebook* (IRDIS, 1985), Appendix A, p. A-1; for 2002, Barry T. Hirsch and David A. Macpherson, *Union Membership and Earnings Data Book* (2003 edition), Table 1b, p. 12.
    *Indicates peak year.

was the position of Old Unionism in 1933, there was doubt that it could ever revive. Professor George Barnett, one of the most prominent labor scholars of the time, forecast in his presidential address to the American Economic Association in December 1932 that:

> It is hazardous to prophecy, but I see no reason to believe that American trade unionism will so revolutionize itself within a short period of time as to become in the next decade a more potent social influence. . . . [W]e may take it as probable that trade unionism is likely to be a declining influence in determining conditions of labor [in the United States]. (Barnett 1933, 6)

Barnett's prediction proved to be egregiously wrong. From that low point, the Old Unionism began the most spectacular expansion since 1886, the year in which the American Federation of Labor (AFL) was established. It expanded throughout the 1930s despite a weak economy and even managed gains during the recession of 1937–38, the only occasion in its history that the Old Unionism increased membership during a business downturn.

Several reasons account for the unanticipated growth of the Old Unionism during the depression years of the 1930s. Public policy was a major factor. Enactment of the National Labor Relations Act (NLRA) in 1935 and its validation by the Supreme Court in 1937 contributed significantly to its growth. The law provided legal protection of the right to organize, shielding workers from employer resistance. This represented a huge step in the evolution of labor law in the United States. Since

1842,[5] workers had had a legal right to join unions but were subject to employment at the discretion of their employers. The NLRA prevented employers from interfering with workers' exercise of their right to organize. Previously, the Railway Labor Act of 1926 and as amended in 1934 had extended these protections to railway workers.

A major contributor to the expansion of the Old Unionism during the 1930s, one omitted in the standard expositions on this period, was the enactment of the Smoot–Hawley tariff in 1930. Because of it, international trade dried up and the American market was virtually closed to foreign competition. When international trade restrictions were reduced, especially in the latter part of the twentieth century, this shrank the size and market share (density) of the Old Unionism.

Another factor that contributed to the unions' organizing success during the 1930s was the New Deal Administration's favorable attitude toward unions. The administration made its favorable attitude toward unions public in several ways beyond enactment of the National Labor Relations Act. For example, in 1937 when the Steelworkers' Organizing Committee—CIO threatened a major strike to unionize the U.S. Steel Corporation, President Roosevelt intervened to persuade the chairman of the board, Myron C. Taylor, to accept collective bargaining rather than fight the union, as the board had in the past. The company then became organized for the first time in its history. Subsequently, Roosevelt appointed Taylor as his personal representative to the Vatican, a major political reward because at that time the United States did not have formal diplomatic relations with the Vatican.

The leadership of the unions was another major factor in their success during the Thirties. John L. Lewis, president of the United Mine Workers of America, understood the opportunities and spearheaded successful organization not only in his own industry, but in others as well. He provided the money and the organizers who facilitated the successful organization of workers. His approach was also far-sighted, in championing the organization of workers based on the industry or company (industrial unionism), rather than craft unionism, the historical organizing principle of the American Federation of Labor (AFL). Although the craft principle was successful in organizing skilled workers for many years in several industries since the inception of the AFL, it failed in the 1920s in the manufacturing industries. Lewis's success led to the establishment of a new federation of organized labor in 1937, the Congress of Industrial Organizations (CIO).[6] It would not be an exaggeration to call John L. Lewis, Mr. CIO. Among the CIO's affiliates were important new unions in auto, steel, and electrical goods manufacturing as well as a few that had formerly been affiliated with the AFL. Manufacturing industries that had historically kept unions at bay became the center of gravity of the Old Unionism and remain so to this day.

The founding of the CIO stimulated competitive organizing and led to bitter infighting between the two federations. The AFL accused the CIO of being infiltrated by Communist, and the CIO charged the AFL with harboring gangsters. Both accusations were truthful to some degree. Lewis, an avowed anti-Communist, nevertheless employed Communists to organize on behalf of the CIO because of their zeal to attack corporate capitalism by organizing workers; thus, a number of CIO affiliates came under Communist influence. This period in the 1930s was also a time when the Communist line from Moscow was cooperation with unions. Later, in 1949–50, because of the Cold War, when some affiliates of the CIO followed the Communist Party line, the CIO expelled eleven of them for being Communist dominated.[7] The CIO chartered new unions to recapture their membership of the expelled unions and was successful in most instances; AFL affiliates also captured members from the expelled unions. However, two unions not only survived the CIO's attacks and some from AFL unions, but they continue to function and remain on the "progressive" political fringe to this day; they are the International Longshoremen and Warehousemen's Union (on the West Coast and in Hawaii) and the United Electrical, Radio, and Machine Workers, who represent workers at GE and some other companies. Even before Senate hearings established links between organized crime and some AFL affiliates, notably the Teamsters and the International Longshoremen's Association (on the East Coast, Great Lakes, and Gulf Coast), these unions' connections to organized crime were well known.

Public approval of unionism was also very strong in the 1930s, and it is commonly believed that this, too, played a role in the Old Unionism's successes of that era. As a result of the organizing campaigns of the 1930s, the Old Unionism rose to peak levels by the outbreak of the Second World War in 1939. Between 1933 and 1939, the Old Unionism added just under 3 million members. After the United States entered the war in 1941, the growth of the Old Unionism accelerated, and from 1941 to 1945, it gained another 3.4 million members. Much of the wartime gain was stimulated by the activities of the National War Labor Board (NWLB). It was established by Executive Order of President Roosevelt in January 1942. The Board was a tripartite agency with representation from management, organized labor, and the public. It was vested with the authority to control wages by compulsory arbitration. The NWLB directly encouraged union membership by authorizing collective bargaining agreements requiring that every worker hired by an employer and who joined or became a union member would be required to maintain his or her union membership for the term of the agreement. These became known as "maintenance of membership" agreements. Under their terms, employers were required to dismiss any employee who did not pay the required dues and maintain good standing in the union for the duration of the agreement. Since "good standing" was determined solely by the union leadership, any worker falling afoul of an officer of the union for any reason could be declared not in "good standing" and would be discharged by the employer at the demand of the union. This arbitrary authority was not remedied until the Taft–Hartley Act of 1947 amended the NLRA. In this regard, it could be said that a union member enjoyed lesser rights with respect to his union than as a citizen with respect to the government of the United States. Because of its activities, it has been said that the NWLB did more than the National Labor Relations Board to promote unionism during the war years.[8] Wage increases granted by the Board were applied generally and were often credited to the union representatives of the Board. Workers associated wage increases with the unions, and this encouraged them to join.

Because of its wartime gains, the Old Unionism's status in American society and its power in the economy became greater than ever before in its history. For example, the Auto Workers' union waged a successful 100-day strike against the General Motors Corporation in 1946. This was in contrast to another major postwar strike after World War I, when the nonoperating railway workers, the shopmen, conducted a national strike against the railways in 1922. That strike involved over 400,000 workers, the largest ever, but within a year the strike ended in the defeat of the unions, although "officially" it did not end until 1928 (Davis 1997).

Shortly after the close of World War II, in a "bookend" to Barnett's gloomy prewar outlook, Professor Sumner Slichter of Harvard predicted a diametrically opposite outlook for the Old Unionism. He argued that because unions had become so powerful, the organized system of labor relations would replace capitalism with a "laboristic society":

> Many kinds of employees are organizing themselves into trade unions, and these unions are the most powerful economic organizations of the time. . . . A *laboristic society* is succeeding a capitalist one. (Slichter 1948, 5; emphasis added)

What did Professor Slichter mean by a "laboristic" society, and what happened to his prediction? Beforehand it should be noted that Slichter's model applied only to the private sector, the Old Unionism, and rightly ignored collective bargaining in the public labor market, at that time a negligible force. Government employee unionism as we now know it, the New Unionism, did not begin until the 1960s (Troy 1994). Slichter argued that the power of the unions over the industries of the country was greater than that of any of the "great 'captains of industry' of previous generations" (Slichter 1948, 5).

The implications of a "laboristic" economy would be, first, that collective bargaining would determine or influence most terms and conditions of employment in the private labor market, and, second, that collective bargaining would allocate economic resources instead of the capitalist system's reliance on markets. In addition to the new strength of the Old Unionism, Professor Slichter could also draw support for his theory from public policy—the National Labor Relations Act of 1935—which fostered collective bargaining, a key building block of a "laboristic society." The enactment of the Labor Management Relations Act (the Taft–Hartley Act) in 1947 amended the NLRA and decreased the power of that law for unions, but it was by no means the "slave labor law," as its opponents sought to depict it, nor could it be credited with preventing the rise of Slichter's "laboristic" society. Slichter's essay was written in 1946, before the enactment of Taft–Hartley. Moreover, the Old Unionism reached new highs in 1953. The Korean War, which began in June 1950 and ended in July 1953, reprised the experience of World War II: unionism and collective bargaining reached new peaks, and in fact density hit a historic high of 36 percent in 1953 (Troy and Sheflin 1985). From this pinnacle, Slichter's prediction would appear to be even more possible. However, 1953 also turned out to be the high water mark of any potential "laboristic society." Finally, it bears noting that Slichter's analysis applied to a predominantly goods labor market, just on the eve of the emergence of a service-dominated labor market, in the 1950s overwhelmingly nonunion.

From Peak to Twilight Zone

During the interwar period leading up to Korea, the Old Unionism leveled off. Daniel Bell, commenting on the condition of unionism, concluded that organized labor had lost its dynamism:

> All these problems of organization, internal politics, and bargaining strategy come to a head at a time when U.S. labor has lost the greatest single dynamic any movement can have—a confidence that it is going to get bigger. Organized labor has probably passed its peak strength. . . . Since 1946 the working population has expanded but union membership has remained stationary. (Bell 1953, 204)

His observation led to what came to be known as the stagnation hypothesis. However, the Korean War temporarily reversed the malaise of the Old Unionism. After the war, density again began to diminish and continued to do so continuously until hitting 8.6 percent in 2002. Thus, the density of the Old Unionism slipped back about one century: at the beginning of the twenty-first century, the Old Unionism stands just 1.6 points above its market penetration rate of 7 percent at the beginning of the twentieth century. Membership, after achieving new peaks in 1956 and 1957, slowly ebbed until revived by the economic stimulation of the war in Vietnam, culminating with its historic record of about 17 million in 1970. Since then, with but two minor exceptions, it has ebbed continuously, dropping by some 8 million members, until reaching its level of 8.7 million in 2002.

Profile of the Old Unionism

Although the Old Unionism of the United States is in its twilight, it remains the largest of its kind among all G-7 countries. That should not be a surprise, given the size of the American labor market; nor is it a contradiction to my assertion that it is in a permanent state of decline. Moreover, the Old Unionism is in decline in all other G-7 countries as well. The degrees and rates of decline vary, as does their position in the twilight zone. Except for France, America's Old Unionism is in the most advanced state of decline and Canada's probably the least. Another fact in its profile is that the Old Unionism in the United States continues to be the dominant wing of organized labor. In contrast, among all other

G-7 countries, public sector unions dominate. In 2002, the Old Union-ism accounted for about 56 percent of total U.S. union membership, the New Unionism accounting for the balance. Early in the new century, I anticipate that the New Unionism will replace the Old as the dominant wing of the American Labor Movement. The current preponderance of the Old Unionism in the United States, compared to foreign labor move-ments, is essential to international comparisons. The standard interna-tional analysis ignores or overlooks the dominance of the Old Unionism in the United States and the dominance of public sector labor in all other G-7 countries. Because of the dissimilar composition of unionism across countries, the standard analyses yield false assessments of what is hap-pening and why in cross-country comparisons (Freeman and Medoff 1984).

Because of the size of this country and its history, the Old Unionism is decentralized, with membership currently in perhaps 35,000 local and intermediate unions[9] spread across all fifty states. In about 1960, there were perhaps 60,000 local unions comprising the Old Unionism. The loss of an estimated 25,000 local unions, through loss of members and mergers, constitutes about a 40 percent reduction of the basic union structure. Second only to membership and density, the loss of local unions very dramatically demonstrates why the Old Unionism is in its twilight. Local unions are the bedrock of the Old Unionism. Unlike corporate restructuring, their reduction is not a rationalization of the structure for more efficient operation, but a loss so severe that it further undermines any expectations of revival of the Old Unionism. The number of organi-zations in the unions' superstructure has also shrunk dramatically. As the membership losses mounted, a number of parent organizations—national and international unions—and intermediate or district bodies have disappeared or merged. The shrinkage of their numbers undercuts the power of the Old Unionism, particularly its trade union function.

The decline the Old Unionism has affected all fifty states (Hirsch and Macpherson 1983 and 2003). Table 1.2, which reports on selected states, shows that the decline in the Old Unionism was greater in states with low union penetration, for example, Texas and Florida, than in the more unionized states. The reasons for this are the growth of nonunion em-ployment and the right-to-work laws that inhibit union membership. New York and Michigan, states with a history of greater union penetra-tion than the average for the country, experienced reduced densities as union employment declined, combined with some growth of nonunion jobs. California has always been less unionized than industrial states,

Table 1.2

Selected States, Densities, 1983 and 2002 (percent)

State	Old Unionism 1983	Old Unionism 2002	Manufact. 1983	Manufact. 2002	New Unionism 1983	New Unionism 2002
California	17.7	10.2	21.0	10.4	43.4	55.8
New York	24.0	15.8	31.0	18.2	69.3	67.6
Michigan	25.3	15.7	46.2	27.3	56.8	54.3
Texas	8.1	3.3	16.1	8.2	18.6	14.9
Florida	7.1	2.8	11.3	3.2	27.4	24.6
U.S.	16.5	8.6	27.5	14.3	37.7	37.8

Source: Barry T. Hirsch and David A. Macpherson, *Union Membership and Earnings Data Book* (1983 and 2002).

mainly because of Los Angeles and surrounding areas, offsetting the high unionization of San Francisco and its environs. Manufacturing, unsurprisingly, shows a similar pattern of decline in Michigan and New York. Michigan stands out with close to half of manufacturing workers organized, and, of course, this is owed to the decline of the Auto Workers' Union in Michigan and New York. The density of the New Unionism in Table 1.2 reflects the national advance of that branch of the Labor Movement. New York had more than two-thirds of public employees organized, but it and Michigan have both lost ground. Meanwhile, the national average over the last two decades has held steady, further evidence that by the end of the last century, the New Unionism had encountered stagnation.

Manufacturing is the epicenter of the Old Unionism's decline and between 1973 and 2002, membership in manufacturing shrank from 7.8 million to 2.4 million (Hirsch and Macpherson 2003, Table 1d, 14)—a shrinkage of almost 70 percent! In 1973 manufacturing accounted for over one-half of the membership of the Old Unionism. With the exception of two years between 1973 and 2002, density in manufacturing has declined annually and was unchanged only once. *More than any other sector of the Old Unionism, manufacturing leads the descent of the Old Unionism into the twilight zone. If a single statistic can document the meaning of the twilight of the Old Unionism, the collapse of its membership in manufacturing is that number.* Without a revival in this industrial sector—none is in sight—there cannot be a recovery for the Old Unionism. Moreover, the nature of manufacturing in what it produces and how it undergoes changes is something the Old Unionism has yet to demonstrate an ability to organize, not only in the United States but in all other G-7 countries.

Significant changes in the occupational-industrial matrix of employment, from blue to white collar jobs, have contributed to the ebb of the Old Unionism. White collar employees have historically been difficult to organize in the private labor market, so as manufacturing uses an increasing number of white collar occupations, organizing becomes more difficult. Projections by the U.S. Bureau of Labor Statistics anticipate that over the decade from 2000 to 2010, employment in manufacturing is expected to grow by 3 percent. Among those that will increase sharply are manufacturing industries that have little if any measure of unionization. Clearly, the future of manufacturing is nonunion, and this underlines the irreversible character of the twilight zone.

Other characteristics of the Old Unionism also point to its descent into the twilight zone. By labor market sector and gender in the year 2000, men and women are far more unionized in the New Unionism than in the Old. Thirty-nine percent of men in the public sector are unionized, compared to 12 percent in the private labor market; women's union participation rate in the New Unionism surpasses their rate in the private sector sixfold, 36 percent versus 6 percent. A similar gap characterizes the union rates among blacks. In the public sector, 39 percent of blacks are organized, as compared to 12 percent in the private sector. Blacks are also slightly more unionized than whites in the public labor market, 39 percent compared to 37 percent, and in the private sector, 12 percent versus 9 percent. Overall, therefore, blacks' union participation rate in the labor market exceeds that of whites. The likely reason for this is that the downsizing that has characterized unionized firms in the private labor market has probably reduced the membership of whites much more drastically than of blacks. Union workers are older than nonunion workers (U.S. Bureau of Labor Statistics 2003), a demographic characteristic that implies an aging Old Unionism, further accentuating its weakness.

Leadership is another problem besetting the Old Unionism. Although unionizing manufacturing is essential to any revival of the Old Unionism, shortly after his election to the presidency of the AFL-CIO in October 1995, John J. Sweeney directed the attention and resources of the Federation not toward manufacturing, but toward agriculture, a sector with notoriously poor prospects for organizing. He announced that organizing some 20,000 strawberry workers in California would be the most important initiative of the AFL-CIO's campaign to revive

and reshape the Labor Movement. The unionization of low-paid agricultural workers has long been part of the folklore of organized labor
and intellectuals supportive of unions. In 1996–97, on behalf of its
affiliate, the United Farm Workers of America (UFWA), Sweeney committed financial and human resources on a scale the likes of which had
not been seen since the organizing drives of the Committee for Industrial Organization and its successor, the Congress of Industrial Organizations in the 1930s. Nevertheless, at the end of the day, of the 20,000
potential members, the Federation and the UFWA succeeded in union-
izing 750 workers (!) (Judis 2001), and these were enrolled only because of the intervention of the Agricultural Labor Board of the State
of California. Like Captain Queeg's query in the *Caine Mutiny*, the
question is, what happened to the strawberry workers' campaign? It
has been speculated that the AFL-CIO spent millions of dollars (the
total has never been disclosed) and committed untold man-hours to
organizing time (Judis 2001). However, the crushing defeat of the AFL-
CIO was scarcely noted in the media and largely ignored by academic
supporters of the unions. From the perspective of the Old Unionism
and its descent into the twilight zone, the strawberry workers' episode
raises questions about both the ability and the accountability of the
union leadership, particularly in contrast to the union leadership of the
1930s. Members pay dues, mostly under the compulsion of a union
shop and check-off agreement, and no questions were ever asked about
the debacle, let alone the willingness of John J. Sweeney and the hier-
archy of the Federation to account for their actions. In any event, the
leader of the Federation is no John L. Lewis.

Rise of the New Unionism

Paradoxically, the rise of the New Unionism beginning in the 1960s can
be considered an indirect outcome of the twilight of the Old Unionism.
It is not an offspring of capitalism and competitive markets, as was the
Old Unionism, and it is virtually immune to the economic factors that
have dealt the Old Unionism such severe blows. Rather, New Unionism
is the product of decisions made by public officials and politicians. To
some extent, these decisions were prompted by the ebb of the Old Unionism and the impact this had on sympathetic public officials and politicians in the 1960s. The decline was creating a gap between the organized
market and the total labor force (including government employment), and
I believe that politicians friendly to unionism decided they could help by

encouraging the organization of public employees, emulating what President Roosevelt had done under the New Deal for private sector workers. Union leaders have always had an interest in organizing government employees, but until the 1960s, political leaders, including Franklin D. Roosevelt, opposed the unionization of public employees. The Wagner Act enacted by his administration to promote unionism specifically excluded government employees from its coverage, including postal employees, some of whose organizations date to the late nineteenth century. Labor organization of postal workers had been sanctioned by Congress under the Lloyd–LaFollette Act of 1912, but could neither bargain nor strike. The Act permitted union membership, but the union had to give up the right to strike. Postal unions finally obtained recognition and the right of collective negotiation under President Kennedy's Executive Order 10988 (Troy 1971). Employees of state and local governments were governed by laws that did not permit or envisage unions and collective bargaining. Federal law could not be applied to them constitutionally in the era of the New Deal, but fifty years later a Supreme Court decision included observations that signaled the power of federal law to encompass them.[10] At the federal level, President Kennedy circumvented the difficulties of obtaining labor legislation for federal employees by issuing an Executive Order. In January 1962, in Executive Order 10988, he initiated the unionization of federal employees in the federal branch of government, with a few exceptions relating to security employees. Governments in many state and local jurisdictions emulated and surpassed the Executive Order in promoting the unionization of their employees.[11] Subsequently, the Carter administration replaced successive executive orders and adopted legislation, the Civil Service Reform Act of 1978, regulating labor relations and collective bargaining for federal employees.

Because of governmental intervention on behalf of unions and in the absence of competitive constraints, in contrast to the bleak record of the Old Unionism, that of the New has been spectacular, at least until recently. For that reason, the two comprise distinct union movements. Affiliation of organizations from each branch of the Labor Movement with the AFL-CIO reflects historic patterns, not commonality of origins in trade unionism. Their closest link is their commitment to political activity, but even so they pursue different as well as similar goals. Differences arise because the two wings of organized labor have different philosophies (Troy 1994). Chapter 4 recounts the origins, development, and philosophy of the New Unionism.

2

WHY IS THE OLD UNIONISM
IN THE TWILIGHT ZONE?

Reasons

The general reason for the Old Unionism's descent into the twilight zone
is explained by Schumpeter's theory of Creative Destruction. The long
downward trend of the Old Unionism, which continued after the stagnation hypothesis was proposed in the early 1950s, indicated that the hypothesis caught only the onset of a much deeper problem; the Old
Unionism went from stagnation to the twilight zone. This movement
indicated that a more comprehensive theory was needed to explain the
continued decline and the absence of any reasonable expectation of a
reversal of the Old Unionism. Schumpeter's theory of Creative Destruction provides this theory; it explains the behavior of the Old Unionism
and why, in part, its downturn is irreversible. Capitalism spawned not
only business enterprise but also private sector trade unionism. Consequently, like businesses, parallel and even identical forces govern the
behavior of trade unions. Schumpeter described the dynamism of capitalism in these words:

> Capitalism, then, is by nature a form or method of economic change and
> not only never is but never can be stationary. And this evolutionary char-
> acter of the capitalist process is not merely due to the fact that economic
> life goes on in a social and natural environment which changes and by its
> change alters the data of economic action; this fact is important and these
> changes (wars, revolutions and so on) often condition industrial change,
> but they are not its prime movers. Nor is this evolutionary character due
> to a quasi-automatic increase in population and capital or to the vagaries
> of monetary systems, of which exactly the same thing holds true. *The*

fundamental impulse that sets and keeps the capitalist engine in motion comes from the new consumers, goods, the new methods of production or transportation, the new markets, the new forms of industrial organization that capitalist enterprise creates. . . . The opening up of new markets, foreign or domestic, and the organizational development from the craft shop and factory to such concerns as U.S. Steel illustrate the same process of industrial mutation, if I may use that biological term, that incessantly revolutionizes the economic structure from within, incessantly destroying the old one, incessantly creating a new one. This process of Creative Destruction is the essential fact about capitalism. It is what capitalism consists in and what every capitalist concern has got to live in. . . . Schumpeter 1975, 82–85, emphasis added)

The Old Unionism, a creature of capitalism, must, like business enterprise, adapt to a process that comprises changes in technology, markets, competition, methods of production, and employment. However, the Old Unionism is incapable of such an adaptation because it is a monopoly, and Creative Destruction and its component forces demolish monopoly power. For this reason, the standard response of the Old Unionism to these dynamic forces is Luddism. Instead of shaping a laboristic society, for the last half-century the Old Unionism has found itself in the grip of Creative Destruction and has paid the price because it can only fight a defensive battle—Luddism. Creative Destruction dismantles monopoly power and has done so to the Old Unionism. Creative Destruction applies only to a limited extent to the New Unionism in the United States. The New Unionism is largely a creature of political action and therefore virtually immune to the elements of Creative Destruction. Consequently, over the same period that witnessed the decay of the Old Unionism, the New Unionism flourished (see Chapter 4).

Specific forces associated with that general theory are structural changes induced by the economy and/or by public policy; increased domestic and global competition—the New Age of Adam Smith; changes in technology; the occupational matrix of employment; the growth of nonunion employment; nonunion workers' aversion to joining unions; and the rapid growth of business enterprise in the United States. Employer opposition to unionism, the favored explanation of the conventional wisdom, is not only exaggerated in its relationship to Old Unionism's decline, but also grossly overstated and misrepresented. Closely related to the argument of employer opposition is the claim that the National Labor Relations Act (NLRA) is also responsible because it does not protect workers from employers and therefore must be amended. Like its denial of the impact of competition on the Old Unionism, the conventional wisdom also ignores the impact of competition on labor law: competition has "repealed" the NLRA. The same analysts also deny, or at least until recently perhaps, that the ebb of private sector unionism is international, contending that few or none of the other G-7 countries have contracted the "American disease" of union decline.

Structural Change—Economic

Structural change encompasses the effects of changes in employment, demography, geography, and public policy on the membership and density of the Old Unionism. Except for public policy, all the other types of structural change are generated by the economy; in contrast, structural changes generated by governmental policy are the product of forces outside the economy.

Economic forces engendered the shift of most employment from the goods to the service sector, the exception being government employment, of which only a small part may be attributed to endogenous forces, while most must be attributed to public policies. The underlying economic force ultimately responsible for economic structural change is Creative Destruction. Its most demonstrable result has been the switch from a goods- to a services-dominated labor market. The shift occurred in the United States during the mid-1950s (Fuchs 1968, 19). It preceded all other G-7[1] countries and by many years. Government services are included in the broadest measure of the shift from goods to services, but if the transformation were measured only by employment in private services, the U.S. lead in the transition would be even greater.

The goods-to-services transformation is one of the essential building blocks to understanding the twilight of the Old Unionism. Even if unions did not lose a single member, the transition would, by itself, reduce the density rate of the Old Unionism. The changeover reduces density because the preponderance of employment in the new service-producing industries is predominantly nonunion. In their acclaimed book *What Do Unions Do?* (1984), Freeman and Medoff appraised the effects of structural change in the labor market on union density and found that it was responsible for 72 percent of the decline in density in the U.S. over a quarter-century period, 1954–1979.[2] Then, they rejected their own results! And why, one must ask. Because the results countered their *preferred* explanation, employer opposition. Further, they contended, the decline was unique to the United States. So, instead of the structural explanation for the decline of union density in the United States, they substituted management opposition. Although they gave other reasons for rejecting the role of structural change in the decline of the Old Unionism, management opposition has always ranked foremost in their joint analysis and in Freeman's solo analyses. For example, "the anti-union management offensive in the private sector is the key to de-unionization of the United States," wrote Freeman, adding that its absence from the public sector explains the successful organization of public employees (Freeman 1998, 79). The disparate behavior between the two sectors, he contended, "constitutes powerful evidence against the structuralist argument that changes in the composition of the work force and jobs from (traditionally union) male blue collar labor to (traditionally nonunion) female, white collar and service labor underlie the drop" (1988, 79). He then proffered what he regarded as the coup de grace to the structuralist explanation: "If *'post-industrial' or structural changes inexorably reduce unionization, density would have fallen in Canada and other developed capitalist countries, all of which have experienced essentially the same structural changes as the United States"* (Freeman 1988, 70, emphasis added).

Freeman and Medoff had previously advanced the same argument in *What Do Unions Do?* and also identified Canada as their litmus test:

> If structural changes were the chief factor behind the decline of unionism, the proportion organized would fall everywhere. . . . Perhaps most telling is the fact that in the country most like the U.S., Canada, where many of the same unions and firms operate, the percentage organized went from below the U.S. percentage unionized to above it. (Freeman and Medoff 1984, 227)

However, their assertions that other countries had experienced the same structural changes as the United States were as wrong as were their international comparisons of unionism. Both the structural and union international comparisons exemplify the familiar comparison of "apples to oranges." The structural changes in the United States not only differed from those in other countries, but they came much sooner than in all the other G-7 countries. Moreover, in the United States, structural change was driven by the growth of private services; in all the other countries it was driven by the expansion of public employment. Freeman and Medoff, and Freeman singly, made a parallel and fallacious comparison of union densities across countries, comparing the *average density of both private and public union membership across countries* (Freeman and Medoff 1984, 281; Freeman 1988, 70, emphasis added). Just like their comparison of labor markets, they ignored the differences in the composition of unionism across all G-7 countries. In all G-7 countries, excepting the United States, well over one-half of union members are in the public sector. Moreover, the public is much more unionized than the private sector. And because the public labor market is *relatively much larger* in all other G-7 countries than in the United States, it size adds statistical weight to the more organized public unionism abroad.

Despite these "apples to oranges" comparisons, not one contributor in the special review of Freeman and Medoff's book accorded by the *Industrial and Labor Relations Review* of Cornell University made any reference to these flaws. Even worse, the authors' pronouncements were mindlessly repeated as if repetition equals reality. Freeman and Medoff's fuzzy math and the host of analysts who echoed their claims resulted from their acceptance at face value of the official governmental data of the other G-7 countries *even though those data fail to adequately distinguish between the public and private sectors* of the labor market and of union membership, as do the American data. If ever there was an example of the emperor's clothes, this is it. Of all the G-7 countries, the most egregious of these errors was the acceptance of Canadian data on membership and employment. In 1999, Statistics Canada, source of the data and the counterpart of the U.S. Bureau of Labor Statistics, began to rectify these faults. However, they have not been completely remedied.

The British have also recently begun to report data on unionism on a private versus public basis, but it is very recent and I cannot comment on its comparability to the American. To date, all historical international comparisons between the United States and the other G-7 countries, with the possible exception of Britain, and that for only a short period, suffer from the same deficiencies as the U.S.-Canadian comparisons. Public sector unionism is more stable across countries because it is the joint product of a labor market sheltered from competition and vigorous encouragement from politicians and public managers. At times the encouragement has been so unequivocal as to equate many public unions as "hothouse" organizations, a term originating among Canadian specialists. If similar encouragement were given by private employers to a favored employee organization in the United States, the National Labor Relations Board (NLRB) would dismantle that organization for being company dominated. Any claim that the growth of the New Unionism is proof of how the absence of employer opposition explains the collapsing Old Unionism misrepresents the relationship of the public employer and many public unions. Even though general quantitative measures of the effects of the goods-to-services changes can summarize the general impact of structural changes, because they are summaries they cannot illuminate the details on what was happening and why. The best illustration of how structural changes affected unionism is to examine manufacturing, the epicenter of the Old Unionism.

The major structural changes within manufacturing over the last three decades have been the substitution of high-tech for older manufacturing industries and technological advances in the older industries. These switches result in associated changes in occupations. Table 2.1 demonstrates that by the beginning of the new century the occupational demands of the new manufacturing industries and technological advances in the older industries were reshaping the workforce of the sector. It is even possible that within a decade most employees in manufacturing will wear "white collars." Analytically, Table 2.1 points up how Creative Destruction is reshaping what economists call the production function: executive and related categories and professional jobs are being substituted for blue collar occupations in the production process. The figures indicate not only how work is changing, but from the standpoint of the Old Unionism and the "twilight zone," a workforce unreceptive or even hostile to unionism is becoming dominant in manufacturing employment.

In contrast to the transformation from goods to services, which automatically reduces density without affecting membership, structural change in manufacturing reduces *both* membership and density. Between 1972 and 2002, while membership in manufacturing shrank by over 5.4 million, employment in manufacturing declined by 3.2 million. Thus, union membership declined one-and-two-thirds as much as did employment, as new nonunion industrial/occupational jobs were substituted for unionized jobs in manufacturing. Could employer opposition account for this, as the conventional view contends? No, the magnitude of the shrinkage is far too large to be explained by that factor. Union loss attributable to employers ousting them from established relationships is minuscule compared to the number of unionized jobs lost. Instead, the decline is attributable to the substitution of new technologies, new industries, and new occupations, and the impact of competition domestically and abroad. Together, these factors reduced the employment of

Table 2.1

Occupational Matrix of Manufacturing, 1972 and 2002

Occupational group	2002	1972
Total	100.0%	100.0%
White collar occupations	*42.8%*	*28.9%*
Executive, administrative, managerial	16.0%	6.2%
Professional, specialty	10.2%	9.2%
Technicians and related	3.2%	—
Sales	4.3%	2.1%
Administrative support	9.1%	11.5%
Service occupation	*1.2%*	*2.0%*
Blue collar occupations	*55.6%*	*69.1%*
Precision, production, craft, and related	18.6%	19.0%
Machine operators, assembly	28.1%	41.9%
Transport and material handlers	3.6%	2.9%
Handlers, cleaners	5.3%	5.3%
Other	0.4%	—

Source: Unpublished data of the U.S. Bureau of Labor Statistics, 1972. Labor Force Statistics derived from the Current Population Survey: Data book vol. 1, 1982.
Note: The occupational classifications became more detailed since the 1972 data; comparability is maintained in the table.

unionized workers and spurred the rapid growth of unorganized industries and occupations within manufacturing. Although the substitution of new jobs provided a large potential market for unions, they could not capitalize on it.

In an account of the decline of the Old Unionism between 1973 and 1998, Farber and Western concluded that "the decline of the union organization rate in the U.S. over the last three decades is due almost entirely to declining employment in union workplaces and rapid employment growth in nonunion firms" (Farber and Western 2001, 480). Their finding is in accord with my previous conclusions, and it underscores the exaggerated claims of employer opposition as the dominant factor, one that Farber in the past had accepted. In general, the sheer magnitude of employment growth and the number of new companies, corporate and noncorporate, increased dramatically, fueling the decline in union density and overwhelming union organizing efforts. The number of NLRB elections in previously unorganized units relative to total private, nonfarm employment dropped precipitously over the last thirty years, and the unions' win rate has averaged just over 50 percent. At the same time, publicly held corporations have undergone rapid changes in corporate behavior and structure to make them more responsive to increased competition. In contrast, many private sector unions are adapting to the new environment by turning away from the private to the public sector labor market to gain new members.

Union avoidance by white collar workers is demonstrated by the record in Table 2.2. From 1990 to 2002, membership and density among white collar employees in manufacturing declined sharply over the twelve-year period.[3] As would be expected, the major loss of membership was among blue collar workers, in particular the skilled (precision workers) and the lesser skilled (machine operators); no occupational category escaped the plunging trend of manufacturing unionism.

The structural changes responsible for the continuing occupational transformation of manufacturing are, as in other industries, the product of the economic lifecycles, secular and shorter run.[4] W.C. Mitchell believes that "once an industry has ceased to advance it soon begins to decline" and over time the life histories of industries tend to become shorter: "an increase in the birth-rate of new products means an increase in the death-rate among old products and a decline in the average life-span of individual industries" (Mitchell in Burns 1934, xvii, xviii).

Similarly, Solomon Fabricant pointed out in his study of manufacturing that in "young industries, whose output shoots up quickly . . . employment [also] expands, most often rather rapidly," and during its mature phase, "an industry's development output expands slowly, if at all, . . . [and] jobs decrease unless the length of the working week is reduced sufficiently to offset the decline" (Fabricant 1942, 146). The exchanges and the replacement of "high tech" for older manufacturing industries have been misrepresented as the deindustrialization of America when, in fact, they constitute the secular changes described and analyzed by Arthur F. Burns, Solomon Fabricant, and Joseph Schumpeter.

Naturally, unions associated with mature and declining industries share their fate. The impact of structural change is illuminated by citing a roll call of unions associated with the rise and fall of industries: Elastic Goring Workers, Carriage Workers, Chandelier Workers, Straw and Ladies' Hat Workers, Stogie Makers, Steel Plate Transferrers, Tip Printers, Glass Flatteners, Sheep Shearers, Mule Spinners, Cigar Makers, Broom and Whisk Makers, Tube Workers, Tack Makers, Sawsmiths, Gold Beaters, Pocket Knife Grinders. Since then many others have joined that list, including what had been the oldest international union in the American Labor Movement, the International Typographical Union.

Table 2.2

Union Membership and Density in Manufacturing, 2002 and 1990
(members in thousands)

	2002		1990	
	Members	Density (%)	Members	Density (%)
Total	2,445	14.4	4,223	20.5
White collar	321	4.5	468	6.1
Executive	52	2.1	50	2.3
Professional	79	4.4	81	4.6
Technicians	58	10.1	86	11.2
Sales	18	2.5	17	2.3
Administrative support	114	7.3	234	10.1
Service	35	16.9	4,816	7.7
Protective services	7	17.1	18	23.7
Service occupations	28	16.9	99	33.7
Blue collar	2,086	21.6	3,663	29.2
Precision	686	21.1	1,066	27.4
Machine	1,025	21.0	1,907	28.8
Transport	169	26.9	302	38.9
Handlers	206	22.5	358	30.6
Other	2	4.8	3	4.3

Source: Unpublished data of the U.S. Bureau of Labor Statistics.

Structural changes have occurred within the private service industries, just as in manufacturing. Again, the United States led Canada and the other G-7 countries in this changeover, as it had in the general switch from goods to services. Of particular significance is the growth of producer service industries: advertising, computer and data processing industries, personnel supply services, management and business consulting services, protective and detective services, legal services, accounting and auditing services, and engineering and architectural services. More white collar occupations are needed to furnish the producer services within manufacturing, as companies continue to provide their own, in-house, services. This contributes to the decline of production in proportion to white collar employment within manufacturing, a development noted above. Likewise, the same development is occurring within the service sector: the growth of producer services increases the share of white collar occupations at the expense of unskilled or lesser skilled service and blue collar jobs within the service sector. Like the changes in manufacturing industries, such internal changes also enhance the sector's resistance to unionism.

Geography is another structural factor affecting density and the comparability of labor markets across countries. The South is and has been the least organized section of the country, and the enactment of right-to-work laws has enhanced the attractiveness of southern states in attracting companies seeking to flee the more organized sections of the country. The desirability of such migration is evident even when the geographic opportunities are limited. British data show a similar internal migration, from more to less organized areas, even in that small country (Bassett 1988; Beaumont 1987, 8–9). The North American Free Trade Agreement (NAFTA) has led some companies to migrate from the United States and Canada to Mexico, but the migration is not as large as often portrayed in the union and general media.

Railway transportation provides an exceptional example of how structural change, not employer opposition, shrank union membership. Unpublished figures on railway unionism that I prepared many years ago at the National Bureau of Economic Research put union membership at 1,075,000 in 1947; the U.S. Railroad Retirement Board reports total employment on Class I Railways for that year at 2,072,000, yielding a density of 52 percent. Over a half-century later, in 2001, unpublished Bureau of Labor Statistics (BLS) figures show 181,000 members, employment of 257,000, and a density of 70 percent. While density rose markedly from 1947 to 2001, membership declined by almost 900,000, and employment by 1,815,000—almost 90 percent!

To explain this paradox, a brief history of railway labor relations is necessary. At the behest of the "standard," or national unions of railway workers, in 1951 Congress amended the Railway Labor Act to permit the union shop and the check-off in collective bargaining agreements on the railways. By requiring membership in the union, these contractual agreements increased union membership and the unions' financial power. These provisions had been excluded from the Amended Railway Labor Act of 1934, seventeen years earlier, *at the behest of the same "standard" unions*. At that time, these unions wanted the union shop and the check-off *excluded* from the Act in order to prevent competitive local, independent unions from benefiting from the union shop requirement. Many of the companywide unions had been established by employers following their victory over the "standard" unions in the railway shopmen's strike of 1922.

Eventually, those local organizations shed any evidence of employer preference and many survived as independent local unions. However, by 1951 the standard organizations had eliminated most of these unions, so with less competition they now wanted the right to negotiate union shop and check-off contract agreements to enhance their monopoly power. At that point, the standard unions persuaded Congress to amend the Railway Labor Act and sanction the union shop and the check-off. These provisions became especially significant when five years later the Supreme Court ruled in *Railway Employees Department v. Hanson*, *351 US 225* (1956) that union shop provisions in railway contracts were not subject to state right-to-work laws, laws that banned the union shop. Thus, the railway unions were given a special exemption not accorded to unions subject to the NLRA, and this solidified their grip on the railways.

States had been permitted to adopt right-to-work laws under the Labor Management Relations Act, the Taft–Hartley Act, of 1947. Despite their legal immunity, market forces nevertheless inexorably reduced railway unionism. Because of structural changes in the labor market—the substitution of other forms of transportation for railways—and increased productivity from technological advances, employment shrank drastically. Meanwhile, the union shop, the check-off, and the standard unions' control over the grievance procedure virtually excluded nonunion employment, unlike what happened in manufacturing, and explaining in part why employment dropped more than union membership from 1947 to 2001. Data for 1994 and 2001[5] also indicate that in those parts of the industry operated by the government (Amtrak), the density rate is significantly higher than in the privately operated and larger freight sector of the railway industry. In 2001, government-operated railways were 93 percent unionized, compared to 68 percent on the private freight hauling. In 1994, the comparable figures were 86 percent densities for government railways and 73 percent in the private. So, over seven years, the unionization rate in the private sector diminished by 5 percentage points, a continuing illustration of the ability of market forces to reduce union power. Another industry, coal mining, paralleled the history of unionism on the railways. It was another highly organized industry in which membership also declined, but unlike railways, its density has fallen sharply since World War II as operations expanded in the open pit, non-union part of the industry.

The rise and expansion of the New Unionism and the decline of the Old Unionism are structural changes *within* the American Labor Movement. These changes also exemplify Schumpeter's theory of Creative Destruction. The share of total membership in the Old Unionism has declined sharply between 1990 and 2002, from over 61 to 54 percent. In

2002, men continued to be the largest proportion of total membership (57.8 percent) and remain the majority in the private sector (over 72 percent). In contrast, women accounted for most members in government (55 percent). Most members in both sectors are white, while blacks account for about 15 percent of total membership, approximately the same proportion in both the private and public sectors in 2002. However, their and the Hispanics' shares of membership, 9.5 percent overall, with 7.8 percent in government and 10.9 percent in the private sector, are not precise because Hispanics are included in black, white, and Asian population groups. The foregoing will not match published estimates (U.S. Bureau of Labor Statistics 2003).

Table 2.3 is a detailed presentation of how much the demographic profile of American unionism changed in just over a decade. It presents the union participation rate (density) by sector, gender, and race in 2002 and 1990.

The general union participation rate (average density) contracted from 16 to 13 percent from 1990 to 2002. However, to analyze the decline, several distinctions—sector and gender in particular—must be noted. Of these the most important is the distinction between the Old versus the New Unionism. The decline was pronounced in the private sector, encompassing the Old Unionism, falling from a rate of nearly 12 percent in 1990 to 8.6 percent in 2002. During that time, membership fell more than 1.6 million, while employment increased more than 1.5 million. This implies that the job growth was nonunion as unionized jobs fell. In contrast, in the public sector, New Unionism rose in both membership and participation rate, accentuating the differences between the two sectors.

Next, demographics reveal the weaknesses and strengths of the two sectors. Women, who have become the larger part of the workforce, have a low participation rate in the Old Unionism, indicating that since AFL-CIO president Sweeney's announcement on becoming president of his intentions to change the profile of organized labor, we have seen the reverse. Small as it was in 1990 at 7.2 percent in the private sector, women's union participation rate had fallen to 5.8 percent twelve years later. Meanwhile, their membership declined by 155,000 and their employment in the private labor market rose by a massive 7.1 million. These cross-currents repeat the analysis that as union jobs were eliminated, they were replaced by nonunion jobs. In the government sector, women's union participation rate rose between 1990 and 2002 from 35 percent to al-

Table 2.3

Union Membership and Density, 2002 and 1990, by Sector, Gender, Race, and Hispanic Origin (membership in thousands)

Sector by gender, race, Hispanic origin	2002		1990	
	Membership	Density (%)	Membership	Density (%)
Total	15,979	13.2	16,776	16.0
Government	7,327	37.8	6,447	36.4
Private	8,652	8.6	10,299	11.8
Men	9,238	14.9	10,597	19.1
Government	3,308	39.3	3,175	38.5
Private	5,929	11.0	7,422	15.7
Women	6,741	11.7	6,179	12.5
Government	4,019	36.6	3,302	34.6
Private	2,722	5.8	2,877	7.2
White	12,829	12.9	13,745	15.4
Government	5,905	38.1	5,268	36.4
Private	6,924	8.2	8,478	11.3
Men	7,612	14.5	8,892	18.6
Government	2,679	9.3	2,611	38.5
Private	4,933	10.8	6,280	15.3
Women	5,217	11.0	4,854	11.7
Government	3,226	37.1	2,656	34.6
Private	1,991	5.2	2,197	6.5
Black	2,441	17.0	2,441	21.0
Government	1,135	37.3	979	36.7
Private	1,306	11.6	1,463	16.3
Men	1,224	18.4	1,366	24.3
Government	493	41.3	441	39.6
Private	731	13.4	924	20.5
Women	1,217	15.8	1,076	17.9
Government	641	34.6	537	34.6
Private	575	9.8	539	12.1
Hispanic	1,513	10.8	1,324	14.4
Government	569	36.1	365	34.9
Private	945	7.6	959	11.8
Men	907	11.4	877	15.8
Government	270	40.5	186	38.5
Private	638	8.8	691	13.6
Women	606	10.1	447	12.4
Government	299	32.8	179	31.8
Private	307	6.0	268	8.8
All Other	574	11.7	467	15.9

Source: U.S. Bureau of Labor Statistics, unpublished statistics. The data are based on the 1990 Census population controls, and therefore data for 2002 will not match published estimates of union membership, which are based on 2000 population controls.

most 37 percent. In this instance, as employment increased by 283,000, union membership rose even more quickly. African Americans have a higher union participation rate than whites in both the Old and the New Unionism, although only slightly more in government. In sum, the union participation rates presented in Table 2.3 evidence the power of structural change in the composition of the Labor Movement.

Public Employment—A Subset of the Shift from Goods to Services

Unlike the general switch from goods to private services, the growth of public employment after World War II, especially during the 1960s, was derived less from the demand of citizens than from politicians. Its impact also had an effect on unionism contrary to that of the switch from goods to private services. While that structural change undermined membership and density in the private labor market, increased government employment facilitated the growth of public employee organization, the New Unionism. Given powerful encouragement from government, and sheltered from competition, public sector unions benefited quickly and extensively from the great expansion of public employment following World War II, especially under the Great Society programs of President Johnson. Public sector unions entered an era of spectacular and unprecedented growth that contrasted sharply with the decline in the private sector over the same period. The relative importance of the two sectors of unions changed radically, the public ascending and the private descending in importance, as portrayed above in Table 2.3.

Structural Change and Public Policy

Ashenfelter and Pencavel (1969) contended that their model of union growth in the United States from 1904 to 1960 was a stable and compact explanation of U.S. union growth. However, a review later concluded that the enactment of the National Labor Relations Act introduced a statistical break in their model—that it was not stable and compact (Sheflin, Troy, and Koeller 1981). The review showed that the NLRA led to increases in unionization, especially in manufacturing, which accords with union history of the 1930s. Similarly, we found a structural break in another model (Bain and Elsheikh 1975), which also claimed a compact explanation of trends in union density in the United States over a similar period. Our findings of a structural break in both models, produced by the Wagner Act of 1935, found that a new regime governed union trends. The transition to the new regime took three to five years, depending on whether one uses the enactment year of the NLRA, 1935, or the year of the Supreme Court's validation of the Act in 1937 as a starting point (Sheflin 1984).

By the mid-1950s, the controlling influence of the NLRA on the growth of the Old Unionism had decayed and a new structural break had emerged (Keddy 1988). Using updated figures from the Troy–Sheflin membership series (Troy and Sheflin 1985), another reexamination of the A-P model reconfirmed the earlier evidence of a structural shift occurring in about 1937. However, it also found another break in the A-P model in 1955. In this instance, the break coincided with the switch from a goods to service labor market. Put another way, market forces overpowered the monopolistic powers bestowed on unions by the NLRA and, in fact, that remains the dilemma of the Old Unionism.

Summary of Structural Change

The cumulative effects of structural change proceeded more rapidly, and their scope and impact were far more extensive in the United States than in all other G-7 countries, setting apart the American labor market from those of all other G-7 countries. Therefore, the structural argument explaining the decline of union density in the United States cannot be rejected on the spurious claim that "Canada and other developed capitalist countries . . . have experienced essentially the same structural changes as the United States" (Freeman 1998, 70). And although the structure of labor markets differs across the G-7 nations, nevertheless, private sector labor organization, the Old Unionism, has declined across all of them, albeit at different rates and at different times (see Chapter 5).

Organizing the Unorganized: Employer Opposition

Employer opposition is the favored explanation of the conventional academic perspective and of unionists to explain the decline of the Old Unionism. But contrary to the conventional wisdom, it is not a major explanation for the shrinkage of the organized system, as already noted. At the same time, conventional usage of the term misrepresents its meaning: Does it apply to existing organized relationships? Or should it be understood as applying only to unorganized workers? Given nearly seven decades of labor relations under the NLRA and even longer under the Railway Labor Act of 1926, as amended, employers in established relationships are rarely able to oust the union representatives of their employees. Decertification elections, permitted by the amended NLRA since 1947, are overwhelmingly won by workers seeking to oust their bargaining representatives, but these cannot be initiated or influenced by employers. And they affect relatively few workers (Troy 1999). The enormous losses that unions have experienced, described in detail above, cannot be attributed to employer opposition; it is quantitatively impossible. Employer opposition does not apply to the losses of the organized system resulting from the disappearance of bargaining units; these occur due to downsizing, for financial reasons, because of plant closings and the substitution of other goods from abroad or from the domestic economy. The misunderstanding of what employer opposition actually means brings up the paradox of why unions were so successful in organizing the unorganized during the 1930s and 1940s, despite the fiercest opposition from employers in the twentieth century and probably in all union history. Indeed, a whole new federation, the Congress of Industrial Organizations, was formed during those years, and manufacturing, historically almost impervious to unionization until those times, became extensively organized in the face of determined employer opposition. Obviously, something new has happened since those years—the factors general and specific as detailed in this book. Employer opposition has always been an obstacle to unionization, and although it may now be more subtle, it is not, to repeat, the principal reason for the ebb of organized representation.

An important deficiency in the explanation of employer opposition to the unions' decline is the presence of *employee opposition* to the organized system. An unstated assumption of the employer opposition explanation is that nonunion workers will join unions if afforded the opportunity—if employers do not oppose their unionization. However, there is a long history of nonunion workers' rejection of unions, as is clearly indicated by unofficial surveys of workers' attitudes and the results of secret ballot elections involving unorganized workers, which are conducted by the National Labor Relations Board. However, rarely do those who attribute the decline of the Old Unionism to employer opposition make the distinction between the two types of opposition. In fact, they contend employee opposition has no independent existence, but is a creature of employer opposition. Employers undoubtedly prefer a nonunion labor relationship, but that preference cannot be easily translated into a result. Ultimately, employer opposition is a marginal reason, not a major one, for the twilight of the Old Unionism. Nevertheless, employer opposition, linked to an ineffective NLRA, remains at the top of the list of union leaders and their academic supporters in explaining unions' decline.

Organizing the Unorganized: Employee Opposition

Employee opposition to unions, as evidenced by polls and NLRB representation elections, while a serious reason for the failure to organize the unorganized, is a blank page in the vast literature of industrial relations. Workers who reject unions are not credited with acumen or independence of thought as are those who support unionism. Yet, if a private poll shows some workers would prefer to have union representation, they are credited with knowledge and independence of thought. Moreover, when workers do reject unions, as they have so dramatically and so often, academics and, of course, unionists mischaracterize this as evidence of employer opposition—intimidation and perhaps brainwashing.

Private surveys of workers' attitudes toward unions tell a different story. I begin with a survey conducted by the Institute for Social Research of the University of Michigan in 1977. Nonunion workers were asked: "If an election was held with a secret ballot, would you vote for or against having a union or employees' association represent you?" (Medoff 1977, Table 4 A, 10). Private sector white and blue collar workers preferred nonunionism by more than two-thirds (67 percent); among blue collar workers alone, 61 percent said they would not vote for union representation, and a much higher proportion, 72 percent, of white collar workers rejected union representation. Although these workers were asked about their preference for organized representation, their response was actually support for individual representation.

Seven years later, in 1984, the AFL-CIO commissioned a study by the Harris Associates on the malaise in which organized labor found itself in the 1980s. The Harris study is by far the most comprehensive ever done to date. The survey was designed to learn the attitudes of nonunion workers toward joining a union. The key question asked of nonunion workers was:

If an election were held *tomorrow* to decide whether your workplace would be unionized or not, do you think you would definitely vote for a union, probably vote for a union, probably vote against a union, or definitely vote against a union? (Harris, Louis, and Associates 1984, Table 20, 63, emphasis added; hereafter cited as Harris)

Sixty-five percent of the nonunion workers replied that they would vote against the union—virtually the same proportion as the Michigan survey reported seven years earlier. The results can be interpreted in the same way: a rejection of organized and a preference for individual representation. Especially noteworthy is the timing of the hypothetical voting. Harris asked if the election were held *tomorrow*, how would you (the nonunion worker) vote? Many critics of NLRB elections had argued that the lapse between an NLRB order for an election and the balloting allowed the employer to influence the outcome. By referring to *tomorrow*, the Harris survey eliminated the possibility of employer tactics delaying workers' decisions, a major criticism of government elections, yet 65 percent said "no" to collective bargaining and "yes" to individual representation. Harris also examined the nonunion workers' past history of voting in these elections and found that most were former union members. Of these, 57 percent had voted for a union in their previous workplace, and 43 percent against. Nearly two-thirds of those who had never been union members said they had voted against the union in their previous workplace. Many of those who had voted for a union in their previous job apparently changed their minds about unions because, in response to a follow-up question, just under *three-quarters* of all nonunion workers said they preferred their present job to remain nonunion.

Henry Farber (a supporter of unionism) combined the results of the Michigan and Harris surveys, and after adjusting for comparability (although he did not adjust for the public/private workers in the sample), showed that nonunion employees' rejection of union representation and preference for individual representation increased dramatically. It rose from more than 60 percent in 1977 to just over two-thirds (67.6 percent) in 1984 (Farber 1989, 10). Later, Farber and Krueger reported a continuation in the rising demand for individual representation, or, as they put it, a continued decline in the demand for union representation (Farber and Krueger 1993, Abstract). The union rejection rate (or pro-individual votes) would have been higher in these surveys if public workers were excluded; they have a much higher propensity to belong to unions than private sector workers (Hills 1985). Currently, government workers' propensity to join unions is more than four times as great as in the private sector, as reflected in their current respective market shares. In the public sector it is 37.8 percent, compared to 8.6 percent of private workers. The National Longitudinal Survey of men in 1980 found that public employees' attitudes are significantly different from those of employees in the private labor market. Among men ages 28 to 38, the only group in which a majority (54 percent) said they would vote for unions were those in government. However, nearly three-quarters (73 percent) of nonunion male workers of the same age range in all industries said that they would not vote for a union in a secret ballot election (Hills 1985). The results of the National Longitudinal Survey reconfirmed the previous surveys on nonunion workers' attitudes toward joining unions.

That high figure of union rejection (or support of individual representation) was repeated in a survey by the *Washington Post* published in 1987 (based on data of 1986). In that survey, the paper asked:

> In the place where you work, if there were an election, by secret ballot, among you and your co-workers, would you vote to form a union?

Seventy-five percent replied no, and only 25 percent replied yes (Perl 1987).

Until the 1990s, the surveys consistently showed that about two-thirds of nonunion workers reported that in a secret ballot election they would not vote for a union. In a May 1993 poll of the public and of union members, the finding of a trend toward nonunionism was attributed "to the desire of employees to speak independently from unions" (Penn and Schoen 1993, 5). The specific question to which respondents were asked to reply was whether employees would rather speak for themselves than through a union. The finding that employees desire to speak independently from unions echoed earlier findings explaining the demand of workers for nonunion representation.

In a 1992 report on the demand of workers for union representation, Farber and Krueger reported: "We find that virtually all of the decline in union membership in the United States between 1977 and 1991 is due to a decline in workers' demand for union representation" (1993, Abstract). Again, translating that finding, nonunion workers preferred individual representation. Nevertheless, the authors rejected this finding in favor of employer opposition. Their rejection recalls Freeman and Medoff's rejection of their finding that structural change could explain most of the decline in density in favor of employer opposition, discussed above.

A 1994 survey included in the final report of the U.S. Commission on the Future of Worker–Management Relations (Dunlop Commission 1994a) reported that 55 percent of nonunion workers said they would vote for a union, 32 percent would vote against, and 13 percent declared they were undecided (Freeman and Rogers 1993). The contradiction between this and all other prior surveys raises doubts in my mind as to its validity. Another survey, completed in 1996, reported that 55 percent of employed nonunion workers would *not* vote for a union, just the opposite of the Freeman–Rogers finding; presumably 45 percent would vote for a union (Lipset and Meltz 1996). Again, public employees were included in these samples, which would affect the results.

It is also instructive to take account of nonunion Canadian workers' response to the same question put to American workers: Would they support or vote for a union in a secret ballot election conducted by the various Canadian labor boards? Canada is of special interest because its workers were believed to be more union-prone than Americans, and because its industrial relations systems, federal and provincial, were patterned after the National Labor Relations Act, but were more pro-union. So for those reasons, it would be informative to discover the attitude of nonunion Canadian workers on the question of voting union or nonunion. Surprisingly, nonunion workers in Canada have rejected unions (favored individual representation) at the same rate as in the United States (Canadian Federation of Labour 1990). In February 1990, the Canadian Federation of Labour (CFL) asked nonunion workers, who came from the private and public labor markets, the following question:

> Thinking about your own needs and your current employment situation and expectations, would you say that it is likely that you would consider joining or associating yourself with a union or professional association in the future? (Canadian Federation of Labour 1990, 3)

Sixty-six percent replied no, and 31 percent said yes, results which virtually replicated the surveys in the United States for similar populations of nonunion workers. Like the surveys of American workers, if the Canadian survey dealt only with private sector workers, the union rejection (pro-individual representation) rate would have been higher. Furthermore, the inclusion of Quebec in the Canadian sample undoubtedly reduced the union rejection (pro-individual) rate, because Quebec is *sui generis* in the Canadian system of industrial relations, or, for that matter, in all political jurisdictions north of the Rio Grande. On the other hand, British Canada more closely resembles the American perspective, so a sample limited to British Canada would have produced an even higher rate of rejection of unionism. The Canadian Federation of Labour was made up of unions that had broken away from the Canadian Labour Congress, the Canadian equivalent of the AFL-CIO, in 1982 over a jurisdictional dispute; the organizations remained separated for about a decade. The CFL subsequently rejoined the Canadian Labour Congress. The CFL's affiliates were primarily building trades unions.

Similar findings about Canadian nonunion workers were turned up by the Canadian Federation of Independent Business (CFIB), an organization of small businesses. The CFIB commissioned the Angus Reid Group, an organization specializing in attitudinal and other surveys in Canada, to examine the attitudes of employees of small businesses in March 1991. Employees of small business were asked: "Would you rather belong to a union or not belong to a union?" For all small business companies, 57 percent of the employees said no, 38 percent yes, and 5 percent did not respond. By size of company (measured by employment), there was an inverse correlation between preference for individual representation and company size: the smaller the company, the greater the preference for nonunionism; and conversely, the larger the employer, the greater the preference for a union. However, in no size group did a majority of employees prefer to belong to a union. The highest preference for unions (companies with 300 or more employees, the largest workplace in the sample) was 48 percent, and this was matched by 47 percent who said they would rather not belong to a union.

In 2002, the AFL-CIO commissioned a telephone survey by the Peter D. Hart Research Associates of workers' attitudes toward joining unions and reported:

> [F]or the first time since 1984 (when the AFL-CIO first asked) half of workers who don't already have a union say they would join a union tomorrow if given the chance. This is a full eight percentage points higher than in 2001 when 42 percent of workers without unions said they would join one. Among all workers—including union members—54 percent say they'd vote for a union tomorrow. (AFL-CIO 2002)

In other words, in 2002 one-half of all nonunion workers said they would not join a union "tomorrow," while 58 percent rejected union representation in 2001. The results imply that the inclusion of union members in the poll increases the percentage favoring union representation by a mere 4 percent! Does this imply that a significant number of unionized workers have only a lukewarm attachment to unionism? The results of the survey are debatable because the question posed was ambiguous. At one point the AFL-CIO's press release reported that workers would join a union "tomorrow if given the chance"; next, it states they would *vote* for a union "tomorrow" if given the chance.

What accounts for the fairly consistent support for individual representation, and conversely the rejection of organized representation, in the United States? The conventional explanation is fear of employer retaliation. However, in the Harris survey for the AFL-CIO in 1984, "fear of employer retaliation" was cited by only 2 percent of respondents—ranking it near the bottom of the list of reasons given by nonunion workers. In the 1986 *Washington Post* poll, 62 percent of the respondents said that fear of employer retaliation was not their reason for rejecting a union. These findings are noteworthy because the 1980s (the Reagan years) were denounced by organized labor and sympathetic academics, among others, as an era especially hostile to unionism. This characterization was also relied on by the Clinton administration when it came into office in 1993, and was a prime motive for the appointment of the Dunlop Commission in the spring of that year for the purpose of proposing amendments to the NLRA.

Fear of the employer has been the public's explanation for workers not joining unions. A Penn and Schoen survey reported that 62 percent of the public believed employer pressure was responsible for the decline of unions; the result demonstrates the effectiveness of repetition irrespective of the facts. Paradoxically, while nonunion workers themselves attributed only a minor role to fear of the employer in their rejecting organized representation, the public and the conventional view give it a major role—and both are wrong. If fear of employer retaliation is not the principal reason for nonunion workers' avoidance of unionism, what are the major reasons? Nearly 60 percent of nonunion workers surveyed by the Harris organization characterized unions as stifling individual initiative (Harris 1984, 11, and Table 7, p. 50). Even 45 percent of union members said the same. Furthermore, 78 percent of nonunion workers told the Harris survey that they believed that their employer was genuinely concerned about them as individuals.

Ninety percent of nonunion workers described themselves as satisfied with their jobs; 51 percent described themselves as very satisfied (Harris 1984, Tables 9 and 11, pp. 52, 54). And as for their treatment by employers, 57 percent of nonunion workers agreed that most employees do not need unions to get fair treatment from their employers. The same percentage also believed that their employer provided all the pay and benefits the company could afford (Harris 1984, 12, and Tables 7 and 19, pp. 50, 62). When individual employees feel aggrieved, Harris also reported that nonunion workers actively used their complaint systems, and often approached management as individuals as well as in groups about work-related issues (Harris 1984, Table 17, p. 60).

A major apprehension among nonunion workers about joining unions is their fear of what I call "the union unemployment effect." To many nonunion workers, union advantages in wage rates are offset by the association of unions with unemployment. To many nonunion workers, the unions' claim of providing job security has been transformed into associating unions with job *insecurity.* Actually, there is an understandable confusion over the term *job security.*

Unquestionably, unions have contributed to preventing arbitrary discharge, and it is in this sense that unions can rightfully claim that the bargaining agreement offers "job security." However, the term is usually equated mistakenly by workers and the public with *employment security.* Actually, nonunion workers have come to equate collective bargaining with *employment insecurity*—the union unemployment effect.

Trends in manufacturing unemployment from 1970 through 2002 show that nonunion workers are not imagining the union unemployment effect. The unions' losses in membership over the last three decades exceeded the decline in employment in manufacturing as noted above. Meanwhile, increases in nonunion jobs largely offset the decline of union jobs. Major reasons for the substitution of nonunion for unionized jobs are technological changes and the higher costs of doing business under collective bargaining. Comparisons of union and nonunion plants showed higher costs in unionized plants coupled with no evidence that the unionized plants could offset the higher costs with advantages in productivity (Kochan, Katz, and McKersie 1986, 103–4; Hirsch 1991; Long 1993).

Is There a Representation Gap?

Unions and union supporters do not concede the existence of employee opposition to union representation. To the contrary, they contend that there is an unfilled demand for union representation, a representation gap. The question of whether this gap exists must be analyzed because a major effort was made by the Clinton administration to prepare and enact legislation based on the belief that such a gap existed. In a word, NLRB election results, which test the actual behavior of workers, say no. By combining all votes against unions in elections in previously unorganized units, surveys show a majority of workers voted against union representation between 1970 and 1997 (Troy 1999, Appendix Table 1, 201). All the surveys noted above, even the AFL-CIO's survey in August 2002, indicate that most nonunion workers do not demand union representation. Nevertheless, academics supporting the union cause claim the existence of a gap in representation.

Until the 1990s the conventional pro-union academic representation gap was identified as consisting solely of workers who demanded, but did not have, *union representation.* However, the definition of the gap began to expand as nonunion workers failed to fill the postulated unfilled gap by voting union. Paul Weiler, probably the leading exponent of the concept, redefined it to include mandatory works councils (Weiler 1990, 282). Following up on Weiler's proposal, and to establish the existence of the gap, Freeman and Rogers (1997) set out to survey the gap. They asked: (1) How do employees think their employers treat them? (2) What are the employees' attitudes toward current workplace organization and human resource practices? (3) Most importantly, what are employees' attitudes toward different forms of workplace participation and organization (a stealth question about union representation)? Their survey was conducted during 1994–96 and is known as the Workplace Representation and Participation Survey (WRPS). As readers may conclude from my comments to follow, my acronym for their survey should be the term *warped.* In brief, the message of WRPS is that workers in the private economy want some form of organized representation, whether by unions, by works councils, or by an undefined independent organization to fill the representation/participation gap in the American workplace (Freeman and Rogers 1997, 31). And the reason this demand goes unfulfilled—no surprise—is employer opposition (pp. 22, 31). Freeman and Rogers, along with many others, have been riding these twin hobby horses for the past two decades. Like its numerous predecessors on the unionized gap, this report is a conclusion in search of a rationalization. Nevertheless, I will briefly review it because it still represents the conventional viewpoint.

The report's first two questions were preliminary to the third (all cited above). And that led to the authors' three "core" questions: "Do employees want *greater* [emphasis added] participation and representation [in decision making] at their workplace than is currently provided?" (p. 8). Thus, the survey began with a biased assumption, for the question asks do workers want a *greater* role in the governance of their work. Their finding was yes—again no surprise—and the authors found it to be the case for a "vast majority." Wouldn't it have been not only logical, but free of bias, to ask, first, if employees wish to participate at all in workplace governance, desire no change, or wish to participate less in workplace governance? Although these questions were not asked directly, in fact, the authors did find, despite the question as framed, that more than *one-third* (35 percent) would keep their role in the workplace unchanged, 1 percent wanted less influence, and under two-thirds (63 percent) wanted *more influence* in workplace decisions. In manufacturing, they reported, the demand for more influence rose to 72 percent. But is "influence" the same as *participation and representation*, their original criteria? To recall, their specific question asked: "Do employees want greater participation and representation at their workplace than is currently provided?" (p. 8). A search of dictionaries and thesauruses did not equate "influence" with "participation," or "representation."

Furthermore, these findings are confusing, and even contradictory. Thus, the attitudes of the minority desiring no change (35 percent) are inconsistent with the finding that 79 to 81 percent of those surveyed, before being queried about specific "sorts of decisions" made by their employers, were satisfied (very satisfied and somewhat satisfied) with the degree of their influence in the workplace (p. 8). After the survey identified specific subjects on which employees might wish to exercise more influence, those reporting satisfaction (as just specified), now ranged from 67 to 81 percent (p. 8). As to how much influence employees desired, the reader is asked to accept such characterizations as "having a lot of influence" and "a lot of direct involvement" (p. 9) as the groundwork for changes in public policy toward labor relations.

Freeman and Rogers also wanted to know how nonunion, nonmanagerial employees felt about employee involvement programs (hereafter

EI), that is, employee participation programs, as structures to improve productivity or quality of output. A total of 86 percent of the respondents found them effective (very effective and somewhat effective). However, in assessing the responses on EI's effectiveness, the authors wrote "only" 31 percent rated them highly, and "only" another 55 percent viewed them as somewhat effective! Yet, they omitted the adverbial qualification when describing the 11 percent of employees who found the EI programs "ineffective" (p. 9). Significantly, Freeman and Rogers did not, apparently, inform their respondents that at the time of the survey, EI programs were under a legal cloud: the NLRB had declared several of them illegal, and a final judicial decision remained in the offing. If the surveyed employees had known this, would they have expressed less support for EI programs, or on the other hand regard the Board's actions as politically motivated?

As to employees' voice in the workplace, Freeman and Rogers found that 85 percent were employed in companies with an open door policy that enabled them to tell upper management about immediate supervisors, but that "only" 28 percent regarded their companies' voice system as very effective, while 49 percent judged it somewhat effective—a total of 77 percent who regarded the companies' voice system effective, and 21 percent who characterized the system as not effective.

With reference to *individual* employee's voice in the workplace, the authors reported that 74 percent of employees rated their employers' "open door, town meeting, and the like" policies (p. 15) as effective (very and somewhat effective), with 19 percent classifying them as not effective and 7 percent not responding. However, even though employees saw value in their employers' policies of voice both for the workers as a group and as individuals and approved of their EI programs—in other words, that they had considerable voice in the workplace and access to management—Freeman and Rogers's "broad conclusion . . . was that most American workers want more involvement and greater say in their jobs" (p. 18). To that end, the authors enlarged the unfilled gap of nonunion workers' demand for voice, representation, and power to include *any form of representation*, whether by union, works councils—referred to as joint committees (shades of the 1920s groups set up by employers)—or an undefined independent organization (Freeman and Rogers 1997, 10, 24). Evidently, they had given up on union organizing as the way of filling the representation gap.

The barrage of academic and union demands for the reunionization of the American workplace developed enough political momentum to lead to the establishment of the Commission on the Future of Worker–Management Relations (Dunlop Commission 1994) by the Clinton administration in 1993. Its operating theory was that a more union-friendly labor law in the private labor market would rebuild the Old Unionism. Specifically with respect to the representation gap, the Commission recommended the legalization of employee participation programs, probably with the expectation by most of the Commission members that these would evolve into unions. However, Douglas Fraser, the union representative on the Board, dissented. He regarded EI programs as barriers to union organization and doubted they would evolve into unions. As for increasing productivity, he argued that union–management cooperation was the proper way to achieve that goal. Employee participation programs had been established by employers in order to foster productivity and eschewed any functions in employee representation. However, the Clinton majority of the NLRB ruled several of these programs to be in violation of the NLRA and disestablished them, that is, wiped them out. At this writing, there has not yet been a ruling of their legality by the Bush-appointed Board or by the Supreme Court. The Dunlop Commission's legislative recommendations were buried at the proverbial last minute, when the Republicans gained control of Congress in November 1994, a month before the Commission's recommendations were issued (Dunlop Commission 1994). Republicans have retained control ever since, making pro-union labor law reform even more remote. The Republicans have introduced legislation to legalize employee participation programs under the National Labor Relations Act with the proposed Teamwork for Employees and Managers Act (TEAM Act) of 1997. The proposed legislation followed a previous attempt that failed because it was opposed by the administration, and this one, too, faced a veto, because organized labor opposed the bill, and the administration enforced Labor's wishes. In view of the Fraser dissent in the Dunlop Commission's recommendations (Dunlop Commission 1994), this is hardly a surprise. However, it is surprising that Freeman and Rogers were silent on the proposed TEAM Act, since Freeman as a member of the Dunlop Commission (and the WRPS report followed the work of the Commission) favored employee participation programs. Perhaps Freeman and Rogers were silent because the Republicans proposed it and knew that organized labor opposed such legislation.

For the sake of argument, even though I regard Freeman and Rogers's findings tendentious, let us assume that they are correct in their finding that a "vast majority" (p. 8) of workers demand more participation and representation in decision making in their workplace than is currently provided. Two questions follow: How many does a "vast majority" of employees translate into quantitatively? And, whatever the number, does it matter in the real labor market? For answers, I turn first to an earlier report of the authors on nonunion employee representation (Freeman and Rogers 1993), and to the May 1994 Fact Finding Report of the Dunlop Commission (Dunlop Commission 1994a).

In their discussion on nonunion representation in 1993, Freeman and Rogers claimed that the representational gap could number 80 million wage and salaried workers! To quote them: "As many as 30 to 40 million workers without unions say they want unions, and some 80 million workers without unions, including many who disapprove of unions, want some form of collective voice" (Freeman and Rogers 1993, 38). At that time, in 1993, 77 million workers were nonunion in the private sector (Hirsch and Macpherson 2002, Table 11c, 12). Later, the Dunlop Commission's Fact Finding Report estimated half that number, 40 million private nonunion workers, plus another 9 million union workers, wanted to participate in decision making at their workplace but lacked the opportunity to do so (Dunlop Commission 1994, 52, and note 33, p. 52). In its final report, the Commission stated, now in relative rather than absolute terms, that the representational gap consisted of "sixty-three percent of employees say they want more influence, compared to 35 percent who are content with things as they are" (1994a, 64). Despite the Commission's claim that the WRPS is an academic work "independent" of the Dunlop Commission, it is evident that there was interaction, not only because Freeman was a member of the Commission, but also because the Commission acknowledged the ongoing work of Freeman and Rogers on the subject.

Is there a "representation gap" in the real labor market? Economists have long distinguished between "demand" and "effective demand," the former being a wish while the latter expresses a consumer's willingness to purchase a product or service at various prices. The difference between the two is the difference between a fanciful wish and an action. The authors recognized this distinction, calling it the "[Ross] Perot Poll Phenomenon," which they explained meant "people saying something sounds good without knowing its content" (Freeman and Rogers 1993, 28–29). Again, assuming their finding of a representation gap is accurate, how is it to be closed? In *Who Speaks for Us? Employee Representation in a Non-union Labor Market*, the authors wrote that "democratic principles argue for their establishment" (Freeman and Rogers 1993, 65), but how and by whom is not explicitly stated. However, I believe it is correct to assume they meant government. This admonition is absent in the later WRPS. As previously noted, Paul Weiler (counsel to the Dunlop Commission) had already urged *mandatory works councils*, only he made no bones about it. Weiler wrote, "it is necessary to take away from the employees (and also the employer) the choice about whether such a participatory mechanism will be present," and, furthermore, employees must be given the right "*of internal participation in a specified range of decisions in all enterprises*" (Weiler 1990, 282, emphasis added). According to Freeman and Rogers, the benefits of works councils would outweigh their costs, as they claimed the experience of Western European countries and Japan demonstrate (1993, 14, 66). However, high Franco-German unemployment rates, lower productivity, downsizing, and the export of production to other countries including the United States, Scotland, and in Eastern Europe can be traced, to an important extent, to the works councils (and unionism) that Freeman and Rogers extol and urge this country to impose on its own workplaces. Meanwhile, the so-called representation gap is continuing to grow as the Old Unionism slides deeper into the "twilight zone" for reasons I address in the next chapter.

Deindustrialization or Deunionization?

Because of the decline in investment and production worker employment in manufacturing, some analysts called Old Unionism's decline the "deindustrialization" of the American economy (Bluestone and Harrison 1982). However, the term is a misnomer. It implies a long-run absolute loss in manufacturing output. If that characterization were accurate, it would translate into a decline of the share of manufacturing to the total output of the economy. However, the real value of output (the current dollar value of output deflated by price changes) originating in manufacturing has been stable over the last half-century. Deindustrialization was, like employer opposition to unions, a favored explanation for the decline of unionism in manufacturing. Although some industries have been in great difficulty, the sector as a whole has done well. Its share of the gross domestic product in real terms has held steady (Kutscher and Personick 1986). The complex movements of the marked decline of manufacturing's share of total employment—the absolute decline in production worker jobs accompanied by the stability of manufacturer's share of real output—are explained by the compensating effect of the sector's gains in productivity. The growth of white collar jobs and new products reflects the same force. Such a performance can hardly be described as the loss of the industrial base.

But indeed, there has been a transformation in manufacturing. Instead of deindustrialization, there has been extensive *deunionization of manufacturing*. But this has not come about from the ouster of unions. Instead, it has been the product of employment growth in the newer and other nonunion sectors of manufacturing, accompanied by the decline of the unionized sectors, as discussed above. Some nonunion companies in unionized industries have been undergoing rapid technological changes in response to global competition, and, in the process, have either maintained or increased employment. The nonunion minimill steel companies are examples. The nonunion movement was also extended to the unionized auto manufacturing companies, all foreign owned. Japanese and more recently German producers who have moved to this country operate nonunion not only in traditional nonunion southern states, but in states with substantial rates of unionization, such as Ohio (Honda).

A comparison of union membership and employment in manufacturing demonstrates that the sector experienced extensive deunionization rather than deindustrialization. Statistical data show that from 1973 to 1998 (at the height of the deindustrialization argument), union membership in manufacturing dwindled from 7.8 to 3.3 million, a loss of 4.5 million in population. On the other hand, employment declined far less, from 20,108,000 to 19,961,000, a decline of less than 150,000 (Hirsch and Macpherson 1998; U.S. Bureau of Labor Statistics 1999). This result demonstrates that the decline of employment in the unionized industries was offset by gains in the nonunion industries and companies. The density rate in manufacturing currently (2002) stands at 14.3 percent, compared to 38.9 percent in 1973 (Hirsch and Macpherson 2003, Table 1d), clear evidence of the extensive deunionization of manufacturing.

3

WILL THERE BE A TURNAROUND OF THE OLD UNIONISM?

In his acceptance speech after being elected president of the AFL-CIO in October 1995, John J. Sweeney stated, "[W]e begin today to build a new AFL-CIO that will be a movement of, by and for working Americans." President Sweeney went on to pledge:

> [W]e're going to spend whatever it takes, work as hard as it takes, and stick with it as long as it takes to help American workers win the right to form themselves in strong unions . . . to organize every working woman and man who needs a better deal and a new voice. Our commitment . . . is to revitalize the labor movement at every level and to change its face to represent the faces of all American workers. (Bureau of National Affairs 1996)

The Issue and the Answers

My answer to the question asked by this chapter's title, and my assessment of John Sweeney's pledge to organize and revitalize organized labor, is that there will be no turnaround of the Old Unionism, and that his pledge has already demonstrably failed. After seven and a half years, union membership in the private sector had fallen almost 770,000, or more than 8 percent, and density had declined from 10.3 to 8.6 percent. In the public sector, membership rose by 400,000, or 6 percent, and density remained flat, 37.7 compared to 37.8 percent (Hirsch and Macpherson 2003, Table 1f, 16). Most unions in both sectors are or were affiliates of the AFL-CIO over this time period. The failure of Sweeney's stewardship, especially following his forecasts, has not yet led to any challenge to his leadership, such as the one he personally led against his predecessor, Lane Kirkland, in 1995, following previous years of union decline. Only in academia would such failure not only be tolerated, but also engender fulsome praise, just as has greeted John Sweeney. In business, such failure would either unseat the chief operating officer or the enterprise would fail. Academia and unions are exempt from these competitive challenges.

How to Revive the Old Unionism—According to the Unions and Their Supporters

Pro-union academics and union leaders have concocted a salmagundi of nostrums to reverse the Old Unionism's descent into the twilight zone, but these boil down to two plans—organizing the unorganized and amending the NLRA. My conclusion is that neither proposed remedy can or will make a difference, even if one or both were feasible.

In 1996, shortly after the election of John J. Sweeney to the presidency of the AFL-CIO, the Federation and the Cornell University School of Industrial and Labor Relations sponsored a major conference in Washington, D.C., to address the ebbing fortunes of the Old Unionism (Bureau of National Affairs 1996). They agreed that the Old Unionism was in a crisis because of its declining membership and market share, and they agreed, too, that unions' problems stemmed from employer opposition, attacks from the Republican Congress, and an adverse legal climate. Unmentioned was that Clinton had been president since 1992, that the National Labor Relations Board was dominated by pro-union members, and that no adverse legislation had been enacted by the Republican Congress, which, in the event, would have been vetoed by Clinton. Indeed, Clinton had, at the behest of the unions, vetoed legislation that would have given legislative approval for employee participation committees.

The conference's goal was to find ways to reverse the decline and increase the membership and density of organized labor. About thirty-five papers were prepared for the meetings by union staffers and university professors. In addition to the primary problem, as they saw it, of how to overcome employer opposition, the conference also devoted its attention to the organization of women and low-wage workers. In a backhanded acknowledgment of *employee* opposition to organization, the conference noted that workers' attitudes about unions and organizing had to be addressed. Thus, there was one recommendation that organized labor needed more research on the attitudes of unorganized workers toward unionization. A major reason for employee opposition, unacknowledged by the conference, is the union unemployment effect. Studies of unions' wage-lifting power are numerous, but those on their impact on employment are not. One exception concluded that "successful unionization of production workers leads to significant declines in employment and output in manufacturing plants" (LaLonde, Marschke, and Troske 1996, 155).

In discussing ways to revive unionism, the conference's attention was drawn to low-wage workers, especially farm workers. This group has always been a favorite of academics, the media (one can recall Ed Murrow's television series), and some in organized labor because its organization would fulfill their ideals of economic and social justice. In focusing on this group, however, the participants ignored the history of organized labor, a history replete with failures to organize the low-skilled, and, on the other hand, success founded on the unionization of the skilled, or craft workers, which lay the foundation for the modern American Labor Movement, the establishment of the American Federation of Labor in 1886, and the rise of the Congress of Industrial Organizations in 1937.

The conference's attention to low-paid workers led to the Federation's effort to organize 20,000 strawberry workers in California, a campaign that ended in disaster (see my discussion in Chapter 1) (Judis 2001). The campaign cost the AFL-CIO millions of dollars (it was said that the Federation spent $95,000 a month during the campaign) (Judis 2001), and went beyond the strawberry fields of California, encompassing rallies and marches around the country. To mobilize its supporters, the AFL-CIO organized rallies and press conferences at the Washington, D.C., headquarters of the Federation, featuring speeches by Sweeney and by leaders of the National Organization for Women (NOW), and the National Association for the Advancement of Colored People (NAACP) (Villarejo 1997). As part of its corporate campaign, the AFL-CIO pressured supermarkets to support better wages and working conditions in the fields. Several agreed; among them were Ralph's, with 408 Southland stores, the sixth largest supermarket in the nation, Gristede's and Sloan's supermarkets with 62 stores in Manhattan, and Key Food with 130 outlets in New York City. The corporate campaign also sought to uncover "dirt" on the targeted strawberry growers. An investment company that managed union pension funds bought control of the largest strawberry grower and then informed the workers that it was not opposed to the Federation's organizing campaign.

For all their efforts, the Federation and the UFWA succeeded in union-izing only 750 workers of the 20,000 (Judis 2001), and these were en-rolled only because of the intervention of the State of California's Agricultural Labor Board. Even though the organization of low-paid agricultural workers would have fulfilled the social and political dreams of so many in the media and in academia, the defeat of the AFL-CIO in this case was virtually ignored. This treatment is in marked contrast to the plaudits given by the same groups to the Teamsters in their strike against the United Parcel Service, or the professional engineers' union in its strike against Boeing, which was thought to herald a revival of the Old Unionism. Actually, neither strike was an attempt to organize new workers, but instead were over new contracts, and they yielded no in-creases in membership.

The fiasco of the strawberry workers also demonstrated the failure of the top-down technique of organizing, in this instance with the Fed-eration itself taking the lead. Perhaps in reaction to the top-down ap-proach, the "bottom-up" approach was later advocated. Actually, this method has historically been the most practiced and reliable. After apparently abandoning reliance on labor law reform and works coun-cils, Freeman asserted:

> The lesson from the depression experience is that bottom-up employee-driven bursts of union activity rather than particular laws are necessary for any resurgence of union density. Another lesson is that any resurgence of unionism will come suddenly, probably surprising the cur-rent crop of experts and labor historians as much as the depression spurt surprised Barnett and other observers of the period. (Freeman 1998, 288)

However, bottom-up activity has shown little success, as demonstrated by the continuing decline in members and density in the private sector, so there has been no parallel to Barnett's mistake at the depths of the Great Depression. This was yet another in an array of recommendations for overcoming the decline that Freeman and others have made to orga-nized labor; all have failed. More than a decade earlier, in the 1980s, Freeman, together with many other academics, advised the Federation to adopt what came to be known as the Union Privilege Benefit Pro-gram. The program was to be offered to nonunion workers as an induce-ment to become associate members, with the hope or expectation that they would join as members and persuade fellow workers to sign up. For a small fee, nonunion workers would be given access to benefits including attorney fees at reduced costs, reduced life and accident insurance costs, participation in a motor club, car repair, travel club services, a Walt Disney World hotel discount, a parent's college advisor, reduced cost for educational books and software, advice on mortgages and real estate, and a dental program. Of course, the program was made available to union members as well. A number of affiliated unions adopted similar programs. In 1995, the Federation added a credit card to the program; it was issued by Household International, from whom the AFL-CIO received $75 million each year for five years ending in 2000. The card had no annual fee and low monthly interest charges. How the Federation spent the sums it received from Household International is unknown.

The attractive benefit package failed to halt or reverse the ebb of the Old Unionism from its inception because, I believe, the nonunion workers who might have been attracted may not have been concentrated in a single company or workplace; in other words, the associate members would more likely have been spread across an area and not constituted a critical mass. The addition of cyberspace benefits, which have since been added, is unlikely to make a difference either. In fact, it could be counterproductive after candidate members, union members, and union retirees became familiar with the enormous number of news sources on the Internet; the unions' position on bargaining and political matters will face competition from these sources. A recent example of union members resorting to an employer's website occurred during the strike of the Screen Actors Guild and the American Federation of Television and Radio Actors in 2000 against the advertising industry. According to the attorney for the Association of National Advertisers, 50,000 of the Guild's 135,000 members had checked out the managements' positions on the issues (residual rights for commercials). As the *Wall Street Journal* commented: "Finally the individuals on all sides of a labor dispute have a chance to make judgments based more on facts and information they consider relevant, not only on the sermonizing of management and union leaders." The event also marked, as the *Journal* said, "the first labor war waged to a significant extent on the Internet" (*Wall Street Journal* 2000, p. A26).

Returning to the Federation–Cornell conference of 1996, Sweeney told the participants that, in contrast to the recent past, new strategies and tactics were required to succeed. That reference was an overt criticism of his immediate predecessors at the Federation, Lane Kirkland, the second president of the Federation, and George Meany, its first president. Among Sweeney's new strategies and tactics was a call for an increase in spending on organizing, perhaps recalling that spending had been a key ingredient of the successes of John L. Lewis and the CIO in the 1930s. However, Sweeney added that simply spending more money would not itself be enough, as, indeed, the failed effort to organize the strawberry workers proved. In addition, he called for more research by the Federation and its affiliates and by academics to increase organized labor's knowledge about workers and employers.

The conference also attacked employee involvement programs (or employee participation committees) designed to improve efficiency in a company. These programs began in the 1970s and became important during the next two decades as employers implemented ways to compete in the New Age of Adam Smith. The NLRB voided a number of these during the Clinton administration, ruling that they were dominated by employers and therefore violated the National Labor Relations Act. According to research presented during the conference by a professor from the Cornell School of Industrial and Labor Relations, these programs impeded union organizing campaigns and caused lower win rates in NLRB representation elections. He also found it extraordinary that the Commission on the Future of Worker–Management Relations, the Dunlop Commission (which was generally regarded as sympathetic to unions), recommended modifications of a section of the National Labor Relations Act (Section 8[a][2] that would result in easing barriers against the employee involvement programs, provided they were coupled with other Commission recommendations to facilitate organizing. I agree that employee participation programs are a barrier to unionization: they provide workaday communications between employers and employees and, at the same time, enable the company to compete more successfully in a global economy because the programs increase productivity. These advantages make employment, higher wages, and related benefits available to workers.

Union attendees at the Conference recognized the crisis facing the Old Unionism, as demonstrated by one leader who proposed abandoning, when necessary, one of organized labor's historic and fundamental principles— each union's claim of exclusive jurisdiction to organize a specified category of workers. He argued for abandoning that principle in favor of a general jurisdiction to organize—in other words, to enroll— new members irrespective of craft or industry. Not only has the "general union" approach failed previously, as the experience of the Knights of Labor in the late nineteenth century demonstrated, but if adopted it would open internecine struggles over jurisdictional claims like those that divided the AFL and the CIO in the 1930s and 1940s. Apparently it received no support and nothing came of the proposal, but it was indicative of the desperate search for remedies.

As noted, the Conference focused on employer opposition. As evidence of its pervasiveness, one participant called attention to the large number of unfair labor practice charges against employers filed by unions with the NLRB every year. Factually, that is correct. Analytically, it is naive. The numbers have indeed increased over the last several decades of the twentieth century, but they are not a measure of the importance of employer opposition or a reason for the decline of the Old Unionism. The filing of charges is a function of many factors besides alleged illegal employer actions. Surely some are legitimate charges of employer violations of the NLRA, but the volume itself is not evidence of the significance of employer opposition. The increase is also a function of the size of the expanded labor market and the number of firms in the economy, so that the population of employer targets has grown. Charges against employers are also a function of unions filing charges as a substitute for losing or preparing to hedge a loss in a representation election, or simply filing to harass an employer.

LaLonde and Meltzer found that employer opposition had only a marginal impact on the fate of unionism and bargaining in the United States (LaLonde and Meltzer 1991). They pointed out that the importance of the number of unfair labor practice charges filed against employers in the United States is exaggerated. The reasons are that the section of the National Labor Relations Act under which illegal employer practices are classified included *unrelated illegalities*, that the number of charges against employers grew because of the growth of employment and because the jurisdiction of the NLRB was enlarged. Curiously, some years after identifying illegal employer opposition as the principal cause of union decline in the United States, Weiler wrote that "most employers still do fight within the legal rules of the contest" (Weiler 1988, 7).

In view of the failure to organize the unorganized in the traditional ways—organizing drives coupled with strikes and NLRB elections—pro-union academics have proposed several substitutes for traditional unionism, all of them versions of what I call *stealth unionism*. All share the goal of getting unionism and collective bargaining across an unorganized employer's threshold. The institutional forms of stealth unionism are the company union, distinguished from its ancestor, the company-dominated union, employee participation committees, minority union representation, and works councils. The resuscitated company union would be established by employee votes—a special NLRB election, I presume—and be limited to special functions, which is mysterious to me because any activities would likely be ruled by the NLRB as encroaching on the functions of a legal bargaining representative and therefore violating the law. The origin of this proposal probably is a practice known as nonunion employee representation. Actually, this practice was banned in the United States in the 1930s. It was exported to Canada and now is being proposed for reexport, with modifications, to this country. Proponents of nonunion employee representation begin with the company-dominated union, legal in Canada because of historical quirk.[1] Presumably, at some point these were converted into local independent unions, organizations legal in both countries. Even so, its proponents claim a distinction from the local independents, which to me is a distinction without a difference. The standard unions always are on the alert to absorb such organizations. In any event, however nonunion employee representation is construed, it has no future in the revival of the Old Unionism.

In its final report in 1994, the Dunlop Commission endorsed the legalization of employee participation committees, provided that it was coupled with a continuation of the prohibition of company-dominated labor organizations. Nevertheless, it drew a dissent from Douglas Fraser, the labor member of the commission, who insisted that the historic ban not be weakened by legalization of employee participation committees, that the ban remain as a bulwark against any form of representation other than standard unions.

The next form of stealth unionism is minority union representation. Under this proposal, a union would be allowed to represent a minority of workers in a workplace. Not only would this proposal contradict the theory and practices of the NLRA and the NLRB since their enactment in 1935, it would reverse union demands from the inception of the law— until perhaps now—that the law must countenance only one representative in a workplace, the representative of the majority. That concept is exclusive representation. When minority representation, on the basis of proportional representation, was practiced for a brief period by the Automobile Labor Board in 1934–35 by its chairman, Leo Wolman, it was denounced as anti-union. Now, history is being stood on its head with the demand for minority representation from those who had always opposed it. Their purpose, of course, is to insert the union into the work-place and, once in, to convert its status from a minority to a majoritarian position. It is akin to the union tactic of "salting" a workplace with co-vert union sympathizers as part of an organizing drive. Thus far, how-ever, the proposal appears to be more academic than one seriously regarded by the more practical-minded trade unionists. They can envi-sion the nonunion position overcoming the union minority as employ-ers find themselves able to deal separately with the two groups.

Works councils are yet another form of stealth unionism. Like minor-ity representation, works councils would be a way station toward union-ism. As noted in the previous chapter, more than a decade ago Paul Weiler, apparently out of desperation in the face of continued union decline, proposed mandatory works councils (Weiler 1990, 284). The probability of works councils in the United States, compelled or negoti-ated, is nil.

Unions have been urged to expand their traditional means of recruit-ing by turning to cyberspace (Wilcox 2000, 268). In fact, the use of cyberspace has been advanced as "a bold plan for organized labor to remain strong for many decades to come" (Shostak 1999, 1). Cyberspace consists of new techniques of communications—e-mail, websites, com-puter networking, cellular phones, fax machines, and video conferencing. Recently, it was estimated that two-thirds of employees in medium and large companies have access to the Internet and the proportion continues to grow (Gindin 1999). Employees communicate extensively with one another and with management for business reasons, and they also e-mail each other for nonbusiness purposes.

But is the future of unionism in cyberspace? My answer is both *no* and *yes*. It is *no* when looking to the future of *trade unionism*, which would consist of organizing either white collar workers, those most likely to have access to the Internet, and blue collar workers, who presumably have less access. My answer is *yes* when looking to the future of *politi-cal unionism*. My answers are applicable to the short and long run, and to both the Old Unionism and the New Unionism. Analytically, I find no reason for cyberspace to reverse the downward trend of the Old Union-ism and believe it can have only a negligible effect in spurring the growth of the New Unionism.

My analysis of the future of *political unionism* reaches two conclu-sions: First, that organized labor's huge investment—ideological, finan-cial, and in-kind—in presidential and congressional elections since the advent of John J. Sweeney to the presidency of the AFL-CIO in 1995, combined with the political activities of the nation's largest union, the National Education Association, which is independent of the AFL-CIO, has diluted Labor's trade union function of organizing the unorganized. And, second, that the Democratic Party, the party of choice of the union leadership and the recipient of organized labor's immense political support, has become the de facto Labor Party of the United States (Chapter 6).

The central question for organized labor's *trade union function* is, does high-tech communication improve the traditional methods of organizing and lead to increases in union membership and density? The traditional methods of organizing are house calls on the unorganized, which I call the "infantry" approach; salting, or inserting union organizers into workplaces surreptitiously to motivate unionism, which, as I have just noted above, is akin to minority representation as a means of organizing; reliance on labor law, that is, charges against employers of unfair labor practices, based on employees' use of cyberspace to organize; public relations, that is, publicizing the identities of companies that resist organizing campaigns or thwart bargaining as "unfair"; exerting pressure on third parties, consumers, and related businesses in order to coerce employers into accepting unionism; and embarking on broad geographic sweeps, such as the ill-fated "Operation Dixie" aimed at the textile industry in the South after World War II. To repeat, the question is, can cyberspace supplement traditional organizing techniques and initiate a surge of unionization in the short or long run? A corollary to organizing the unorganized is, can cyberspace complement or add to the power of the unions' ultimate battle tactic, the strike?

My response to all these questions is no. In contrast, a leading advocate of the power of cyberspace to rejuvenate unionism projects a visionary and aggressive acronym, FIST, to encapsulate its potential. Separately, F represents "futuristics," I "innovation," S "services," and T "tradition" (Shostak 1999, xvi). The elements of FIST are themselves devoid of aggressiveness, but collectively they imply a fighting, not a cooperative model in labor management relations, a *sine qua non* in this, the New Age of Adam Smith. However, perhaps the sum of the parts *did* intend to imply an attack mode for organized labor. Perhaps, too, there is also an intended echo of the film *F.I.S.T.* (Federated Inter State Truckers), which was about the Teamsters and Jimmy Hoffa, whose aggressive organizing efforts made the union the largest in the country for a time.

An advertised advantage of cyber organizing is the computer's ability to create a "virtual union presence" for the target audience, the nonunion worker. I compare its symbolism to the historic emblem of the unions' presence, the union label. The AFL created the label early in its history and promoted it through its Union Label Department, now the Union and Service Trade Department of the AFL-CIO, to inform members and the public which products are union made and therefore should be bought for that reason. The cyberspace equivalent consists of flyers, announcements, cartoons, and other electronic messages that acclaim the unions' ability to raise wages, improve working conditions, provide a grievance procedure, inform the workers of their rights under the law, bundled with the e-mail addresses of the organizers, thus offering a package that the nonunion worker should buy. Advocates of cyberspace as an organizing tool have singled out women as likely to respond to the virtual union label, although no specific advantages to women are set forth (Shostak 1999, 200–4). Most women who are organized are employed by government and became union members primarily because of policies that fostered the organization of public employees, rather than responding to special advantages for women; the same explanation applies to minorities, suggesting that cyberspace tactics are not necessary (Troy 1994). In 2002, minorities, women, and, for that matter, men are far more unionized in the public than in the private sector. Women's union participation rate in the New Unionism surpasses their rate in the private sector more than sixfold: 36.6 percent versus 5.8 percent. A similar but smaller gap characterizes the union rates among blacks. In the public sector, 37.3 percent of blacks are organized compared to 11.6 percent in the private sector. Blacks also are slightly more unionized than whites in the public labor market, 39 percent compared to 37 percent, and in the private sector 12 percent versus 9 percent (see Chapter 2). Overall, blacks' union participation rate exceeds whites. The likely reason has been the downsizing of unionized firms in the private labor market, which I believe reduced the membership of whites much more drastically than that of blacks.

Statistically, the "virtual union" in cyberspace has been no more successful in organizing workers than the union label was in persuading union members and others to purchase union-made goods. The expectation that cyberspace would be a contrivance powerful enough to reverse the decline of union density and membership of the Old Unionism and checkmate the New Age of Adam Smith clashes with experience. In the

United States, density has declined continuously for a half century (since 1953), and membership for three decades since 1970, except for minor gains in two years during the 1990s. Current statistics on unionism, private polls, and NLRB election results demonstrate that most nonunion workers continue to prefer to remain nonunion (Troy 1999). Moreover, the decline of the Old Unionism is not unique to the United States; it extends to all the other G-7 countries, and this indicates that causes common to all countries are responsible for the common infirmity (Chapter 5).

While cyber organizing has failed on a macro level, that is, it has not led to *general* gains in unionism, on the micro level the question remains, has it led to the unionization of the *new* occupations generated by the new technologies? Examples of the occupational groups engendered by cyberspace that would be targets of cyber organizing are computer systems analysts; engineers; computer programmers; applications and systems software designers; specialists in data processing, preparation, and information retrieval services, including online databases and Internet services; designers of integrated systems, and developers and managers of databases and onsite computer facilities. In the private sector, few of these occupational groups have become unionized. Instead, cyberspace organizing has typically organized the traditional occupations, as illustrated by newswriters. Although the organization of a few online newswriters and columnists is regarded by some as evidence of successful union forays into the new cyber occupations, reports by the union with jurisdiction over these occupations, the American Newspaper Guild and its parent organization, the Communications Workers of America–AFL-CIO, actually contradict the claim. The Guild has asserted that these occupations are simply an extension of its historic jurisdiction—that *writers*, whether they write code or edit text, are *writers* over whom the union has historically had jurisdiction. Based on this claim, the Newspaper Guild has won jurisdictional recognition from some managements. On the other hand, other managements have opposed the inclusion of online writers in Guild bargaining units (Fitzgerald 1998), because they *do* regard online writers as a new occupational group, one produced by cyberspace. Paradoxically, the "futuristic" attitude of management toward the use of cyberspace (a building block supposedly only for unions) is served by that outlook. This doubtless makes it more difficult for the unions to organize because of management claims that online writers are outside the Guild's jurisdiction; in this exchange, count an advantage of cyberspace to employers. More importantly, management has used cyberspace to communicate its position toward workers independent of the union's filter.

Union efforts to organize specific groups of white workers, some of them high-tech, have typically failed, as illustrated by the following. The Communications Workers of America (CWA) attempted to organize 400 customer service representatives at Amazon.com in Seattle, while other unions attempted to organize about 5,000 other Amazon employees in eight distribution centers across the country in 2000–2001. Amazon employees were said to be upset with management for several reasons: the prospect of the company moving its customer service jobs to New Delhi, India, and the decline in the value of employee-held stock options. How joining a union and collective bargaining can reflate the value of stock options is puzzling, to say the least, because studies of the effect of collective bargaining on the prices of publicly traded securities uniformly conclude that they reduce stock prices (Hirsch 1991 and 1991a; Freeman and Medoff 1984). In the end, the unions lost. When Amazon announced that it was shutting down the Seattle service center as part of widespread cuts in January 2001, it also killed one of the few nascent efforts to unionize tech workers. Other closely watched efforts that died in 2001 included those at online grocer Webvan and online electronics reviewer Etown.com, both of which ended when the companies went out of business. The same labor leaders who hailed those efforts in the beginning stages have now mostly given up on trying to organize high-tech workers.

Had the CWA achieved representation status, the union said that it would negotiate "wage floors," which would amount to from 30 to 40 percent of total compensation, rather than the exact terms of wages (Greenhouse 2000). To me, this proposal promised prickly issues for individual workers, not to mention the union, suggesting that the union's bargaining stance would be a risky scheme. The use of wage floors recalls the system of payment-by-result, which also relies on minimums and which has had its difficulties in determining wages even when the product is tangible, as in the garment trades; when the output is a service, wage determination on this basis would become even more challenging.

Meanwhile, opponents of global competition have argued that cyberspace could resuscitate the nineteenth-century Marxian call for the workers of the world to unite against their employers and free trade! They believe that high-tech communications could organize international

coalitions of workers and other disaffected people who share anti-
capitalist ideologies, modeled on the Industrial Workers of the World
of the last century (Hackenberg 2000). Nominally still in existence,
the IWW declares:

> The IWW is a union for all workers, a union dedicated to organizing on
> the job, in our industries and in our communities both to win better
> conditions today and to build a world without bosses, a world in which
> production and distribution are organized by workers ourselves to meet
> the needs of the entire population, not merely a handful of exploiters. . . .
> Since the IWW was founded in 1905, we have recognized the need to
> build a truly international union movement in order to confront the glo-
> bal power of the bosses and in order to stand in solidarity with our
> fellow workers no matter what part of the globe they happen to live on.
> (IWW homepage)

The "new" IWW has united with other groups, including representatives and members of unions, to demonstrate against the World Trade
Organization (WTO) in Seattle (Hackenberg 2000), against the World Bank
in Washington, D.C., in April 2000, and since then elsewhere in the world.
Ironically, these opponents of the New Age of Adam Smith would apply
cyberspace, a contemporary and futuristic technology, to social and economic concepts already "consigned to the dustbin of history."

The impotence of cyberspace in the Labor Movement's trade union
function is also evident in the strike record. In the United States there
has been a sharp and continuing decline in strikes over the last several
decades, and in the 1990s strikes hit all-time lows in frequency, duration, and, to a large extent, effectiveness. Paradoxically, cyber communication may prove of greater value to employers than to unions, an
alternative not considered by its proponents (Shostak 1999). Cyberspace
enables employers to present their side of a dispute directly to the workers without the union filtering their position, thereby weakening the
union's power to strike and to bargain (*Wall Street Journal* 2000). Under the law, employers' right of free speech is protected as long as that
speech contains no threats of reprisal or promises of reward.

While cyberspace fails as an organizational device, its use raises questions of privacy, issues that have not been addressed either by its advocates (Shostak 1999, 40) or by the American Civil Liberties Union
(ACLU). To the contrary, the discussion praised the accumulation of
private information. The detailed personal information on employees

gathered for the purpose of organizing may or may not have been obtained with the consent or knowledge of the individuals concerned. Second, to what other uses might that personal information be put? Most important of the alternative uses is political activity. It is a virtual certainty that the unions would use this personal information for political purposes. The union leadership has shown no hesitancy in using members' dues and fees, most of which are collected by compulsory contractual agreements, to support political goals and candidates of *their* choice, irrespective of many members' and fee payers' political preferences to the contrary. The unions' leadership has also levied political assessments on members without a referendum. So why should they hesitate to use personal information gathered in the course of an organizing drive for political purposes?

Cyberspace cannot overcome the decay of the Old Unionism because its causes are embedded in the fundamental laws of demand and supply inherent in conditions such as freer markets at home and abroad, the principle of substitution, technological changes in production, and structural shifts in the labor market. These same market factors have also "repealed" public policies to promote and sustain unionism among all G-7 countries. The most notable example is Canada, and in particular the province of Quebec. New evidence of the impact of markets on employment and unionism has recently appeared in the U.K., the mother country of modern trade unionism. Notwithstanding the Labour government and its pro-union policies, unionism in the private sector has diminished. Meanwhile, new and sharp reductions in employment and unionism are taking place in key bastions of British unionism, auto and steel manufacturing. Market forces—overcapacity relative to demand, competition, and the exchange rate between the British pound and the euro—have severely reduced auto manufacturing. Faced with a worldwide overcapacity, auto producers sharply reduced production and employment. About two years ago Standard and Poor's forecast that manufacturers in the U.K. would produce at an annual rate of 2.2 million cars by 2004; now, however, that estimate has been reduced to 1.6 million, a cutback of more than 27 percent. To counter higher costs, manufacturers began shifting production to cheaper locations outside the country. The U.K. is being hit disproportionately by these moves because many facilities in the country are old and inefficient. The sterling/euro rate of exchange parallels the experience between the United States and Canada in the 1980s (Troy 2000). In addition to financial factors, British unions believe that the U.K.'s legal system facilitates the layoff of workers because British law does not require consultation with employees and unions before jobs are eliminated, as does European, especially German, law (Champion 2000).

An important nonmarket factor hampering the organizing of workers, one studiously avoided by unionists and academics in assessing the causes of union decline, is the quality of the union movement's leadership. In my judgment, the contemporary leadership falls short of those who led unions during the decades of the 1930s and 1940s, and that deficiency has contributed to the unions' failure to successfully practice their trade union function. A parallel failure in the business community would lead to the resignation of the corporate leadership and their prompt replacement, or the demise of the enterprise. In contrast, managerial failure in the Labor Movement is hailed as heroism in "battling against the odds" and rewarded by infrequent challenges and repeated reelection. It has been reported that John J. Sweeney, president of the AFL-CIO, intends to run for reelection despite the fact that unionism is now at a lower ebb than when he took office in 1995. Although he had once promised a "youth movement" in leadership of the Federation, that promise has been forgotten—without protest; indeed, it is hailed by his peers in the Labor Movement. Moreover, he also intends to include Secretary-Treasurer Richard Trumka in his reelection bid, despite the fact that Trumka once faced federal criminal charges for his role in the reelection scandal of former Teamsters president Ronald Carey and took the Fifth Amendment. The Federation's rules *require* any officer who takes the Fifth to be dismissed from his job, but Sweeney waived the requirement for Trumka.

In contrast to the private sector, cyber organizing would appear to be useful in enrolling the new high-tech occupations in the government sector. But this is illusion rather than fact. There are many union members with high-tech occupations in the New Unionism, but this is the result of the *unique* history of unionization in the public sector. In fact, organizing in the U.S. public labor market currently confronts stagnation, and its penetration ranks well below that of all other G-7 countries. Can cyber organizing make a difference? I doubt it, because the traditional methods of unionization and cyberspace played virtually no role in the growth of the New Unionism in the United States.

Cyberspace has generated no new labor law either theoretically or empirically. Instead, existing legal dicta have been extended to cover employees' use of e-mail, just as predicted by Circuit Judge Easterbrook (Easterbrook 1996). Theoretically, "the courts and the Board scrutinize the promulgation of otherwise valid workplace rules for evidence of intent to interfere with protected rights" (Robfogel 2000, 4). The evidence would include the extent to which the establishment of employer rules on the use of cyberspace comes in the wake of organizing activity or the spirit in the adoption and enforcement of these rules (Dolin and Rozmus 2000). NLRB policies on employees' use of employers' e-mail system are derived from Board and Supreme Court decisions dating from the 1940s (Bureau of National Affairs 2000). The salient points are as follows: Where employees spend most of their working time on computers, their work space is treated as equivalent to the conventional concept of employees' work area and therefore subject to extant Board rules and Court decisions protecting the rights of workers under the NLRA. Accordingly, employers may ban the *distribution* of organizing information during working time and in work areas. The rules on *solicitation* are more nuanced: The employer can ban *solicitation* to join a union by e-mail on working time because it could interfere with production. During nonworking time, an employer may not totally ban solicitation, but could partially prohibit e-mail solicitation in computer work areas. For example, an employer may prohibit mass mailings, chain mail, spam, and the like (as distinct from one-on-one e-mailing, which is analogized to conversations), because such computer usage is likely to be disruptive and interfere with production, and may often overlap with the working time of various recipients. Therefore, employer rules banning solicitation must be selective, not total. Once a union becomes the bargaining representative of the employees, the Board's long-held authority to determine which subjects are subject to collective bargaining will apply to the use of cyberspace: "There can be little doubt that employer policies on e-mail and computer use are also mandatory subjects of bargaining" (Robfogel 2000, 6). An important unresolved issue that is likely to be addressed in the future is whether employers, who have the technological ability to block incoming e-mail, may restrict incoming nonbusiness messages. Another might be to require that "[u]nder certain circumstances, the Board should *require* employers to provide the names and addresses of employees where the organizational structure, including the computerized workplace, deprives employees of access to each other" (Wilcox 2000, 268). The dispersal of employees away from a central workplace because of cyberspace may justify a legal requirement that employers furnish the union with employees' names and addresses. One analyst believes the Board has been leaning in that direction (Robfogel 2000, 14). However, the Bush administration's appointments to the Board may alter this prospect.

Although I argue that cyberspace will not reverse the downward trend in membership and density, nor materially assist collective bargaining, it *can* augment the already immense political contributions of the union movement in political activity. Cyberspace is used to rally members to political meetings, encourage registration, and, of course, turn out the vote. Moreover, it is an important aid to the electoral prospects of the Democratic Party, the Party of choice of the leadership of the Labor Movement.

Labor Law Reform

The alternative to reviving the Old Unionism, since organizing has failed, is to make the National Labor Relations Act more union friendly. Before examining specific recommendations, any reform would nevertheless fail in reversing the steady fall in the Old Unionism. The reasons are both conceptual and empirical. The conceptual reasons are embedded in the New Age of Adam Smith—increased competition domestically and internationally—structural changes in the labor market, creative destruction, and technological advances. In the competition between the visible and the invisible hand, the visible hand of the NLRA has steadily succumbed to competitive and related forces. The NLRA was a regulatory response to what was believed to be a failure of the labor market in the late 1920s and early 1930s. Over the last half-century, resurgent market forces have been "repealing" that public policy, just as they periodically have done to the minimum wage law and to the Old Unionism. While the employer opposition model has focused its attention on amending the NLRA, it has been strangely silent about the Railway Labor Act (RLA), the other federal policy governing private sector labor relations in this country. If its reason is that the RLA only covers a relatively small number of employees and that union penetration remains at peak levels and therefore does not require their attention, the model should be reconsidered. Empirically, unionism has edged downward even among this group of highly organized workers despite the RLA.

Employer opposition, though typically characterized as if it was some demonic force, is, of course, a dimension of competition. Thus, in a back-handed way, the employer opposition model acknowledges the pervasiveness of the New Age of Adam Smith: employers are acting out market imperatives. The precise issue is the extent to which employer opposition is responsible for the loss of union members as distinct from other competitive forces that reduce the number of unorganized workers. Because of public policy, employer opposition is confined to the unionization of unorganized workers. For this reason, and contrary to conventional views, employer opposition has had little impact either on the absolute decline in union membership or the percentage of the labor market organized. Even Weiler has stated that "[m]ost employers still do fight within the legal rules of the contest," and that "our national labor law still states that employees can have union representation and collective bargaining if they want it . . . [b]ut they must really want the benefits of that institution . . ." (Weiler 1988, 7).

Representation election results show that unorganized workers have a tepid interest in joining unions (Troy 1999). Sifting through the record of these elections from 1973 to 1988, Farber and Western found the following results: That organizing activity had declined "sharply" *prior* to Reagan's defeat of the Air Traffic Controllers' strike in 1981; that there was "little evidence that the changes in the administration of the NLRA later in the decade [of the 1980s] adversely affected the level of union organizing activity"; that their framework for accounting for private sector union decline attributed most of the losses in membership to differential growth rates in employment in the union and nonunion sectors, in which the nonunion sector grew, as the authors put it, "much more rapidly"; and that "changes in union organizing activity had relatively little effect [on the decline]" (Farber and Western 2000, Abstract, and 30). These findings require elaboration. First, the defeat of the Air Traffic Controllers' strike, which occurred in the public sector, was widely blamed for the stiffening of employer opposition to unions, but, as the study showed, it actually had virtually no impact on the NLRB's administration of union organizing in the private sector. As employment expanded in the nonunion sector, unions could not cope with the expansion. Beyond what the authors reported are other facts that illuminate the decline of unions in the period they studied, as well as before and after, namely, the huge losses in membership of the leading unions. Today, the United Steel Workers is a shadow of its former self; the Auto Workers are at about one-half their peak membership; likewise, the Teamsters are at least 750 thousand members down from their record high of 2 million plus. Because of market factors, short and long term, I had anticipated that union penetration of the private sector labor market would fall to approximately the levels prevailing at the beginning of the twentieth century, about 7 percent. In fact, the data for 2002 now put the Old Unionism's market share at 8.6 percent. Put another way, the Old Unionism's density has slipped back almost a century, before there was an NLRA (see Table 1.1, page 4). In a conceptual sense, the Old Unionism in the twenty-first century is operating in a legal environment similar to that at the onset of the twentieth century. Essentially, both the Old Unionism and the labor law that governs it have slipped back a century.

Additional evidence of the impact of market forces on private density, including managerial opposition, structural and economic change, and international trade, is found in other studies. The first concluded that "[t]he primary reason for the large decrease in unionization . . . [in the U.S. from 1973 to 1988] appears to be the shrinkage in size and/or number of *existing* union establishments" (Bronars and Deere 1989, Abstract, emphasis added). Because employers in the United States can do very, very little to oust unions from existing relationships under the law, in contrast to the 1920s and early 1930s, Bronars and Deere's finding illuminates further the impact of structural changes and competition on declining American private density.

They also found that only 13 percent of the decline could be attributed to unsuccessful union organizing from 1973 to 1988. This, too, reflects structural change and offers insights into the scope of employer opposition. It is only in the replacement of new for vanishing union members that employer opposition can effectively come into play. However, that opposition must be legal, not just opposition. Even the harshest critic of employer opposition in the United States, Professor Paul Weiler of the Harvard Law School, has written that "[m]ost employers still do fight within the legal rules of the contest . . ." (Weiler 1988, 7). Juxtaposed to Bronars and Deere's results, the net effect of illegal employer opposition is, therefore, marginal in the dynamics of union organization in this country, the rhetoric notwithstanding. Largely ignored by the conventional wisdom are surveys of nonunion workers reporting their unwillingness to join unions (Farber 1989). As for the contention that employers' strategic policy of locating new facilities in nonunion areas is responsible for union decline (reducing new organization), the disappearance of existing union relationships dwarfs strategic plant location as a factor.

4

THE BRAVE NEW WORLD OF THE
AMERICAN LABOR MOVEMENT

O wonder! How many goodly creatures are there here! . . .
O brave new world, that has such people in't.
—William Shakespeare, *The Tempest*

The Transformation of the American Labor Movement

The American Labor Movement is evolving from a blue into a white
collar labor movement in the United States. In 2002 white collar workers accounted for just about one-half (49.7 percent) of the union population (see Table 4.1), and early in the new millennium they will become a
clear majority. However, this is much more than an exchange of one
occupational group for another as the majority in the Labor Movement.
It signals that organized labor is divided in several new ways: One is the
division between the public and private labor markets. A second is that
government employees dominate among white collar groups. And most
important, within this group are the teachers. Together with other local
public employee unions, the teachers pose a challenge to municipal governance.[1] The challenge is so great that later in this chapter I ask, "Are
Municipal Unionism and Collective Bargaining Compatible with Municipal Governance?" I conclude that they are, but at a price.

The changing composition of the American Labor Movement underlies fundamental differences in philosophy that separate the private, the
Old Unionism, from the public, the New Unionism: The Old Unionism
demands a redistribution of income from private employers to unionized workers. The *Weltanschauung* of the New Unionism demands a
redistribution of the national income[2] from the private to the public
economy for the benefit of unionized public employees.[3] White collar

Table 4.1

Occupational Distribution of Union Membership, 2002 and 1990

Occupation	Membership 2002	Percentage of total 2002	Membership 1990	Percentage of total 1990
White collar[a]	7,947	49.7	7,143	42.6
Blue collar[b]	5,714	35.8	7,536	44.9
Service[c]	2,226	13.9	2,006	12.0
Other[d]	89	0.5	91	0.5
Totals	15,979	100.0	16,776	100.0

Source: Unpublished data from the Bureau of Labor Statistics.
Notes: The summed totals may not match those published by the BLS or those of the table because of rounding.
[a]Includes executive, administrative, managerial, professional, technical, sales, clerical, and support occupations.
[b]Includes protective services and other service occupations.
[c]Includes precision, production, craft, repair, machine operators, assemblers, inspectors, transportation, material moving handlers, cleaners.
[d]Farm, forestry, personal household, and other.

unionism in the private sector will have no role in shaping this philosophy because the *Weltanschauung* of unions is shaped by their market sector, not by the occupation of the members. Moreover, white collar unionism in the private sector is far weaker than its public counterpart; its market penetration is low and narrowly concentrated; it consists to a large extent of professional engineers and technicians in the avionics industry, office workers employed by unions (perhaps its largest bloc of members), some insurance staff, auto manufacturing, sales personnel in supermarkets and department stores, and professional actors. The largest private sector white collar union is the Office and Professional Workers, AFL-CIO, which claims a membership of about 118,000, including 35,000 in Canada, and 221 affiliates (Gifford 2001, 53).

Though the two philosophies conflict, the conflicts rarely surface into open disputes. To be sure, there are important issues where the philosophies agree, notably opposition to free trade. This agreement stems from the shared belief within the American Labor Movement in increased government intervention in the economy and society. Because of the size and importance of public school funding in public spending, the teachers' unions—the National Education Association (NEA) and the American Federation of Teachers (AFT)—are the most important group in pushing for the private to public redistribution of the national income. During this decade, I expect the two will merge and pursue their redistributive goals more boldly. The NEA is already the largest union in the United States with about 2.5 million members, and after the merger the new union will have about 3.5 million members, probably making it the largest in the world. At this time, the NEA is independent of the AFL-CIO, while the AFT is an affiliate. I also expect that as part of the merger agreement, the new union will be an affiliate of the AFL-CIO.

Statistical Profile of the Brave New World of the Labor Movement

Table 4.1 summarizes the evolving transformation of the Labor Movement and indicates that the definitive watershed, when over one-half of all union members will wear a white collar, is imminent. Since the establishment of the modern American Labor Movement near the close of the nineteenth century, marked by the founding of the American Federation of Labor, unionism in the United States has been symbolized by the blue collar industrial worker. However, that historic symbol is now being replaced by a union member wearing a white collar and, as Table 4.2 shows, employed by government, federal, state, or local.

The transformation now under way is the joint product of the growth of white collar and the decline of blue collar union membership. Of the two, the decline of blue collar membership (1990–2002) by more than 1.8 million members was the more weighty factor. The loss took place entirely in the private sector; in contrast, blue collar membership actually *rose* in the government sector (see Table 4.2). Of the gain of 807,000 in white collar union membership from 1990 to 2002, 660,000 were government employees and 147,000 were private sector employees. However, even though white collar workers' membership rose in the private labor market, the participation rate fell to 4.8 from 5.7 percent. This is in line with the continual expansion of private white collar employment and the rate at which white collar workers join unions. Employee opposition to unionism is far greater among this category of workers than among blue collar workers, and given the anticipated growth of employment among white collar occupations, the decline of the Old Unionism's density becomes even more certain.

Before proceeding further, I wish to distinguish my analysis from *The Transformation of American Industrial Relations* (Kochan, Katz, and McKersie 1986). In that book, the authors advocate *a transforma-*

Table 4.2

Union Membership in the United States by Occupational Group and Sector, 2002 and 1990

	Membership 2002 (000)	Density 2002 (%)	Membership 1990 (000)	Density 1990 (%)
Total	15,979	13.3	16,776	16.0
Government	7,327	37.8	6,477	36.4
Private	8,652	8.6	10,299	11.8
White collar	7,949	11.1	7,142	12.1
Government	5,177	36.7	4,519	35.3
Private	2,772	4.8	2,623	5.7
Blue collar	5,712	20.0	7,537	25.9
Government	721	41.7	708	38.9
Private	4,991	18.6	6,829	25.0
Service	2,226	13.2	2,006	14.4
Government	1,394	40.9	1,200	40.1
Private	832	6.2	806	7.4
Other	92	3.4	91	4.8
Government	34	20.5	50	27.2
Private	58	2.3	41	2.4

See notes to Table 4.1.

tion of American industrial relations; they did not offer an analysis of an empirical transformation that was actually occurring—the rise of public sector industrial relations in the economy. Their purpose was to advocate more government intervention in private sector industrial relations in order to rejuvenate the ebbing private sector labor movement. The keystone of their proposed transformation was legal authorization for unions to participate in managerial decisions—an American version of (then West) Germany's system of co-determination. Ever since, academics have continued to advocate an American version of co-determination as a panacea to arrest the decline of the Old Unionism. Unaccountably, the analysis of Kochan et al. ignored the transformation actually under way by that time, the new system of government employee unionism and industrial relations in the United States. In fact, by 1986, the year their book was published, public sector density was more than two-and-half times that of the private sector (Hirsch and Macpherson 2001, Tables 1b, 1f, 12, 16). In contrast to their *advocacy* of a specific change in industrial relations in the private sector, this chapter *reports* and *analyzes* empirical changes in American industrial relations—the emerging dominance of government employee white collar unionism, centered on teachers—heralding the "Brave New World of the American Labor Movement."

While Table 4.2 demonstrates the shift to white collar unionism, and makes it clear that the change is concentrated in the government labor market, it is also indicative of the future. Historically, there had been an expectation that white collar unionism would emerge in the private sector, tracking the unionization of blue collar workers (Kassalow 1966). But it did not and has not. The expectation became a matter of urgency to the Labor Movement in the 1960s as the service-dominated labor market stimulated a huge expansion of white collar jobs in the private market, coupled with the decline of unions in the goods sector. Harry Douty, a veteran observer of union trends in the U.S. Labor Department, observed over three decades ago that "[i]f unionism and collective bargaining are to grow, certainly relative to the 'organizable' labor force, greater penetration into white-collar employment must be achieved" (Douty 1969, 31). As of 1966, Douty reported 2.7 million white collar members and a density of 10.5 percent (p. 33). Certainly, his expectation was correct. Total white collar union membership, density, and collective bargains have indeed increased, but the gains are concentrated in the public economy. Table 4.2 also demonstrates that not the occupation, but the type of labor market, governs trends in unionism. Thus, as previously noted, while blue collar unionism plummeted in the private labor market, it actually rose in the government labor market.

In contrast to government unions' successes in enrolling more members, organized labor's efforts to represent those at the bottom of the economic/skill ladder in the private sector have failed. This was highlighted by the AFL-CIO's (John Sweeney's) failure to organize the strawberry workers, which I have discussed previously and examine in detail below. Thus a marked dichotomy, one might ironically say class distinction, within the Labor Movement is developing between the well paid, whom unions represent, and the lower paid, whom the Federation repeatedly claims to represent. This class distinction is more pronounced and serious than the one that existed during the years when the highly skilled trades of the original AFL were identified as the "aristocrats" of Labor compared to the lesser-skilled union members. For all intents and purposes, that class cleavage vanished with the rise of the CIO. Now, the union class structure has developed a new division, one that I expect to be permanent. At one end are the highly educated and well-paid professional white collar occupations, members on the upper-income/occupational ladder, and at the other, all low-paid working people, whom Sweeney and the Federation regularly and inaccurately claim to speak for, notably when they demand increases in the minimum wage. Those demands actually benefit union workers more, who are above the minimum wage, and less so those directly affected by the law. While the low paid often lose their jobs as a result of this chimerical benefit, wage pressures build to reestablish the wage differentials and related benefits caused by the enactment of the minimum wage—to the benefit of unionized workers. Higher minimum wages also make the lower paid less competitive with union scale. Until the 1930s, organized labor *opposed* minimum wage legislation because it indicated to nonunion workers that they could look to the government for wage and related benefits and therefore did not need unions.

The unions' class dichotomy enhances the already substantial political power of the "upper class" of unionized workers. Most importantly, these are the professional teachers in public education. Politically, the "Brave New World" of the American Labor Movement will be led by middle-class, perhaps I should say upper-middle-class, government white collar workers, not working-class (blue collar) workers. This middle-class leadership, combined with like-minded leaders of blue collar unions, has already converted the Democratic Party into the de facto Labor Party of the United States (Chapter 6).

In contrast to the unionization of the well-paid, white collar union members employed by government, the AFL-CIO's effort to recast itself as the representative of the interests of working people at the lowest end of the occupational/wage level in the private labor market, specifically the 20,000 strawberry workers in California, culminated in disaster. The disaster undermined John Sweeney's forecast that a rejuvenated AFL-CIO under his leadership would change the face of organized labor. Paradoxically, the AFL-CIO has largely ignored a much larger group of low-paid workers, private household workers. In 2002, there were well over 700,000 in this category. There has been no change in the unions' face viewed from the bottom of the occupational visage. However, the "Brave New World" of organized labor, unionism with a professional and governmental face, has developed, a product more of government than of union organization. I will address the origins of the New Unionism later in this chapter and will point out that Sweeney did contribute to the evolution of the New Unionism by transforming a small and unimportant private sector union which he headed, the Building

Services International Union, into a predominantly government workers' union, the Service Employees International Union.

Are Municipal Collective Bargaining and Municipal Governance Compatible?

My answer is yes—but at a price. The unique model of labor–management relations in the public sector, particularly at the local level, prompts both the question and the conclusion. The model differs from the private sector in how collective bargaining is done and its consequences for consumers in the private and public economies. Collective bargaining in government is not merely an extension of the practices and results of the private labor market, as claimed by the conventional wisdom and as typically portrayed in the literature (Freeman 1986). To begin with, the public and private employer are not equivalent because the word "employer" does not capture critical differences between public and private sector entities. What the literature identifies as an "employer" in the public domain is not a clearly identifiable employer as in the private sector. Not only is the public employer endowed with a unique characteristic—sovereignty—the public employer is actually an agent of the taxpayer, who provides the funds for and receives the benefits of public services, but never enters the arena of collective bargaining. The agent alone determines how to conduct and resolve bargaining with its unions.

Paradoxically, conventional wisdom claims the absence of differences between the two sectors, but simultaneously demands reforms in public labor law and practices in order to eliminate key distinctions between them and to make the public model into the image of the private one. At the top of the list of demands is legislation granting public labor organizations the rights of full collective bargaining. Translated, this means giving government unions the right to strike, with a few obvious limitations (such as for police and firefighters), and enlarging the scope of issues subject to bargaining. In public education, the teachers' unions have already gone further than private unions in demanding, through practice as well as legislation, the right to influence, if not to determine, what is taught and how, to the detriment of learning (Lieberman 1997). This power is analogous to having unions explicitly demanding co-determination in how to produce a firm's product or service. Now, it is true that private sector unions implicitly influence these decisions; for example, union work rules do influence if not determine how production is carried out. So, while both sectors have influence in determining how to provide a good or service, they differ in the means and degree of exerting influence. No private sector union has as comprehensive a role in influencing its industry as the teachers' unions do in public education. This explains both the poor results of many public schools as well as the public school authorities' inability to reform poorly performing school districts. If the public sector unions' demands to eradicate basic distinctions in collective bargaining between the sectors were implemented, would the differences between the two labor markets be erased? The answer is no. The differences are greater even than the conventional wisdom's subtle acknowledgment concedes.

Labor–management relations in municipalities and school boards are singularly different from those in the private sector. They are also the dominant form of public sector bargaining because most public employees, over 13.4 million, were employed by local government, as compared to 4.9 million at the state level and 2.6 million at the federal level in 2001 (U.S. Bureau of Labor Statistics 2002). Most local government employees are in the field of education. (Incidentally, total government employment exceeds employment in manufacturing.) Although some organized private industries are also labor intensive, the most important difference in collective bargaining between the two sectors is the *political* dimension of labor–management relations in government, and especially at the local level. At the local level of government, the political aspect of the bargaining relationship is particularly important because of the public employer's political dependence on the union's power, its wealth, and its membership (voters). And this relationship, a relationship of a labor-intensive industry with local politics, leads to distortion of labor costs, as the three major examples identified in this chapter will demonstrate. And by labor costs, I not only mean total compensation, but, in addition, the costs of work rules—in a word, Luddism. Moreover, these work rules create externalities: uneducated children who are ill equipped to compete in America's labor markets, which must be weighed in assessing the effect of the New Unionism on society. Private employers have a much freer hand to resist high direct compensation costs than do public employers. A variety of measures—introducing technological improvements, redesigning work, reassigning workers, promoting based on merit, and introducing merit pay—are much more easily implemented by the private than the public employer, again because of the political component of collective bargaining in government.

Conceptually, the application of these measures puts the compensation of labor in its correct perspective—labor costs per unit of output, the *real* cost of labor. If union work rules thwart productivity, then labor costs per unit of output rise or even soar, as is typically the case in municipal labor relations.

Of course, direct compensation—wages and benefits—plays a direct role in determining the real cost of a unit of production. And in this, organized public employees have a comparative wage advantage over organized private employees. Comparisons of unionized earnings between the public and private workers in the metropolitan areas of New York, Los Angeles, Philadelphia, and Detroit, for example, show that in 2002, mean weekly earnings and mean hourly earnings in constant dollars of public employees consistently exceeded organized workers in the private sector (Table 4.3). These earnings figures apply to workers' principal job and include the usual pay for overtime, commissions, and tips, *but exclude bonuses and nonwage benefits* (health insurance, pensions, and so forth), which are doubtless higher in the public sector.

Table 4.3 is *not* a quantitative comparison of union to nonunion workers assessing the unionworkers' wage advantage relative to comparable nonunion workers. That method *has* assessed which of the two organized sectors, government or private, has a larger relative wage effect, and it has been widely believed that private unions had an edge. But as Richard Freeman argued, in his comprehensive article on public sector unionism in 1986, the relative wage effect of public sector unions was probably understated. The figures presented in Table 4.3 support that judgment—that the wage impact of government unionism is greater than in private sector unionism. The figures in Table 4.3 compare organized public to organized private workers in the Standard Metropolitan Statistical Areas (SMSA), and they show that organized public employees have higher earnings and wages than organized private workers in the same SMSAs. Only in private manufacturing are unionized earnings sometimes greater than those of public workers, and this is because of the additional factors that enhance the wage-lifting power of unions.

Organized governmental workers' wage effects exceed those of organized labor in most of the private sector because of stronger wage rigidity effects: public workers seldom return gains in compensation and rarely concede measures to increase productivity that would offset labor costs. This "immunity" stems from very limited competition, the fact that government is a labor intensive industry, the pervasiveness of

Table 4.3

Mean Weekly Earnings in Constant Dollars of Public and Private Organized Workers in Metropolitan Areas, 2002

	New York City		Philadelphia		Los Angeles		Detroit	
	Earnings $	Union density %	Earnings $	Union density %	Earnings $	Union density %	Earnings $	Union density %
Public	940	67.4	809	54.6	836	57.8	779	54.8
Private	812	14.3	772	11.0	689	10.2	762	17.9

Source: Barry T. Hirsch and David A. Macpherson, *Union Membership and Earnings Data Book*, Table 6a, 36-47 (2002).

Luddism, and the belief that the government's pockets are very deep, if not bottomless. Finally, it is likely that comparisons of compensation between the two sectors fail to take into account the numerous fringes, pensions, holidays, sick leave, and other benefits that are more widespread in the public sector, as illustrated by what I call "The Philadelphia Story," which I will summarize later in this chapter. Not surprisingly, the compensation effects of the New Unionism have contributed to precarious fiscal conditions, and at times even insolvency, in local government. It should be noted that in his comprehensive account of public sector unionism, Freeman (1986) made no mention of the de facto bankruptcy of New York City, which occurred in 1975, a decade before his article, nor of the de jure bankruptcy of the San Jose, California, school district, which had also taken place already, even though both were in great measure the consequence of collective bargaining. In addition, no textbook on labor relations with which I am familiar mentions bankruptcy in connection with collective bargaining in government.

It would be an oversimplification to attribute costly municipal labor relations solely to intractable union demands, or simply to supine public management engaged in collective bargaining. *Instead, it is the political character of the municipal labor–management relationship that is at the core of the financial difficulties of local governments and hinders steps to offset the resulting high unit costs of labor—in short, it is political Luddism.* Not only does the political factor distinguish labor–management relations in the public from the private sector in general, but it gives public employees a comparative advantage over private sector relations in compensation, as Table 4.3 indicates.

In addition, other important conditions of employment—disciplinary procedures, layoffs, and the permanent closing of the establishment—add to the comparative advantage of local government labor relations by adding to unions' wage rigidity and upward-pressing effects on wages. Financial losses may compel a private employer to shut down and go out of business, but municipalities and other public jurisdictions cannot go broke and close down! They may undergo bankruptcies and reorganization, but like the phoenix, they rise again.

The proximity of local public officials to their employees, a proximity that applies particularly to mayors and elected school board officials, makes these officials more vulnerable to the financial pitfalls of collective bargaining. As the late Speaker of the House Tip O'Neill observed, all politics is local, and his insight certainly applies to local public sec-

tor bargaining. Politically ambitious mayors and similar elected officials view bargaining with municipal unions and other local unions as a
cornucopia of opportunity. By fostering union organization and collective bargaining, a mayor and elected school board members create a
political partnership of enormous potential. The political partner, the
union, provides financial and in-kind contributions in elections, funded
by members' dues, fees, and voluntary labor time during elections. Payment of dues may be required, or obtained by agency shop fees. However, ultimately the taxpayer funds the bargaining settlements, and thus,
the taxpayers fund the mechanism that causes them to pay higher taxes
and receive inefficient public services. The compulsory payment of dues
and fees converts the union into a powerful financial as well as political
machine. Politically, it becomes a potent source of financial and in-kind
political support—at no personal expense to the candidate and little to
the party, typically the Democratic Party.

The major adverse effect of local collective bargaining is its impact
on municipal and school board finances. It threatens these institutions
with bankruptcy and, in some cases, imposes it on them. The outstanding examples are the de facto bankruptcy of the City of New York in
1975, and the de jure bankruptcy of the school district of San Jose, California, in 1983. Philadelphia faced bankruptcy, but was pulled from the
brink by the bold managerial leadership of its mayor, Edward Rendell,
beginning in 1992. These examples illustrate three ways in which local
government confronted bankruptcy, and show how municipal collective
bargaining challenged the viability of municipal governance. The examples raise the question "Are Municipal Collective Bargaining and
Municipal Governance Compatible?"

1. The Bankruptcy of New York City, 1975

The City of New York was de facto bankrupt in 1975 when it could not
market its debt, but avoided legal bankruptcy under Chapter 9 of the Bankruptcy Code because of extraordinary measures that had the additional
effect of reducing municipal self-governance. To avoid de jure bankruptcy
under the Code, the City needed to obtain the approval of 51 percent of its
debt holders in order to institute a plan of reorganization. At the time,
there were an estimated 160,000 individuals or families who held $5 bil-
lion in debt and about two-thirds of the outstanding bonds, and many
others were registered in nominee names. Because the debt was so widely

held, it was clearly impossible to secure the required percentage of the bondholders in order to gain approval for a plan of reorganization. Another reason for finding an alternative means for restructuring the City's debts was the Beame administration's (Mayor Abraham D. Beame, 1974–77) desire to avoid the political cost of admitting that financial bankruptcy had occurred on its watch. To avoid legal bankruptcy, therefore, the assistance of the State of New York was enlisted. The State oversaw the City's financial reorganization, essentially serving the role a bankruptcy judge discharges under the Federal Bankruptcy Code. Theoretically, the Federal Bankruptcy Code does not give the courts the authority to act as executive or legislative bodies, but it does permit the courts to interfere with the governmental power of a debtor municipality, its property and revenues. Consequently, the courts de facto have powers and, in these circumstances, exercise the powers of municipal executive and legislative bodies. Hence, the Bankruptcy Code provides a mechanism for curtailing the sovereignty of a municipality when it becomes insolvent. In the case of the San Jose, California, school district, collective bargaining was the sole cause of the district's insolvency, as will be discussed later.

In the New York City case, the State of New York set up an Emergency Financial Control Board (a.k.a. the Control Board, which is still in existence), which included the governor of New York, the mayor, the City and State comptrollers, and three members appointed by the governor. A special deputy state comptroller assists the Board. Effectively, the Financial Control Board took control of the finances of the City of New York. The Control Board began with a financial plan for New York City to cover a three-year period, 1975–78. The Board was given the power to approve all major business contracts, including labor contracts, to estimate revenues and expenditures, and to extend a freeze on hiring through fiscal 1978. The Board also had the power to disburse City revenues after being satisfied that they were consistent with the financial plan. Its powers also covered the City's semi-independent agencies, the public school system, higher education, hospitals, and other services.

To overcome the City's financial exigency, the State established the Municipal Assistance Corporation (MAC), which was empowered to convert the City's short-term debt into long-term debt through a new bond issue—with an attractive interest rate and guaranteed by a 4 percent sales tax, a stock transfer tax, both heretofore paid to the City. In addition, the bonds carried the *moral obligation* of the State of New York. The State Legislature enacted special default legislation shielding the City from creditors for ninety days, coupled with the filing of a financial plan for repayment with a state supreme court. In addition, the Congress of the United States enacted legislation authorizing the secretary of the Treasury to make short-term loans to the City, not to exceed $2.3 billion at any single time.

Major purchases of the MAC bonds were made by the City's five pension funds, notably those of unionized and other workers. Unions trumpeted their investments as demonstrative of their commitment to the City and their civic virtue in saving NYC from a financial debacle, while ignoring their role in putting the City into the crisis in the first place. Their action is reminiscent of the joke in which a person kills his parents and then asks the Court for leniency because he is an orphan. The Board's financial plan worked and the City recovered from that disaster. When Edward Koch was elected mayor in 1978, he adopted plans for financial solvency, but it must be understood that lurking in the background were those emergency measures invoked during the term of his predecessor, Abraham Beame. However, the path to New York City's financial disaster had begun some two decades earlier, under the administration of Mayor Robert F. Wagner, Jr. Under Wagner's administration, the City began the practice of selling short-term bonds to meet current expenditures; Wagner also initiated municipal unionism and collective bargaining in 1957, doubtless in emulation of his father's authorship of the National Labor Relations Act nearly two decades earlier. His action anticipated by five years President Kennedy's Executive Order 10988, which initiated unionism and collective negotiation in the executive branch of the federal government in 1962.

By 1991–92, the City once again lost control of finances under the mayoralty of David Dinkins because of its labor costs and generous welfare benefits. The chairman of the MAC (still in existence) rejected the mayor's proposed five-year budget plan because the City wanted to substitute a $1 billion sale of MAC bonds for real estate tax proceeds—a substitution of long-term indebtedness for current expenditures—a financial practice similar to those that had bankrupted the City. In this instance, the Dinkins administration was seeking a variation on an old theme: substituting long-term MAC bonds, instead of short-term bonds, to meet current expenditures. In reply, the Emergency Control Board demanded that the City reduce its employment rolls. The unions' reaction was that this effectively destroyed the social programs they elected Dinkins to deliver (Purdum 1991)!

Although the immediate cause of the de facto bankruptcy of New York City in 1975 was the financing of short-term needs by bonds, ultimately, a major cause, if not *the* major cause, was the acquiescence to unions' demands for compensation, without the City receiving offsetting gains in productivity. As a result, unit labor costs soared. Even Donna Shalala, later secretary of the Department of Health and Human Services under President Clinton, and Carol Bellamy, at one time president of the New York City Council, attributed New York's financial debacle to the inability of city officials, dating from the mayoralty of Robert F. Wagner through Abraham Beame, to say "no" to unspecified groups. The leading "unspecified groups" were the unions and the welfare clientele, but the two avoided identifying them. At the same time, Wagner and his successors were unable to get what Shalala and Bellamy called a "quid pro quo." The term was a euphemism for agreements from the unions to alter work rules and increase productivity, in contrast to Mayor Ed Rendell's later success in Philadelphia. Who were the unidentified groups referred to by Shalala and Bellamy? Not surprisingly, given their liberal political attitudes, the word "unions" never appeared in their analysis, nor did the City's costly welfare system. Most of Shalala and Bellamy's analysis focused on the loss of revenue—the tax base. As might be expected, they diagnosed the real problem as one of insufficient tax revenue (Shalala and Bellamy 1976).

But the mismanagement of the City's finances was not the only cost imposed on the City and perhaps not the most severe. Clearly, the role and practices of the Financial Control Board undercut municipal sovereignty. The special arrangements to avoid de jure bankruptcy transferred political power from democratically elected municipal officials (however incompetent) to an appointed administrative board. Even Shalala and Bellamy described the transfer of authority from the City's elected officials to an appointed board as "a program of governance" that "eliminated the last vestiges of fiscal home rule of the City" (Shalala and Bellamy 1976, 1128). Technically the City did not go belly up, but can it really be said that the governance of New York City has been the same ever since—with State supervision lurking in the background? Clearly, municipal collective bargaining exacted a toll on municipal governance and procedures; the results establish a definitive distinction between municipal and private bargaining, and for that matter, even between municipal and public sector bargaining at the state or federal levels of government. Localized collective bargaining is sui generis.

2. The San Jose School District Case, 1983

The case of the San Jose, California, school district is the second of the three models of response by a local governmental jurisdiction to bankruptcy in which unions and collective bargaining were responsible in whole or part. Collective bargaining saddled the school district with high-wage costs that it could not sustain. In contrast to New York City, the San Jose bankruptcy, largely attributable to local collective bargaining, was resolved under the Federal Bankruptcy Code of 1937. In 1983, the school district became financially insolvent: it could not meet its debts for telephone and water utilities; nor for the wage increases it had contracted to pay its employees, mostly teachers, its largest obligation; nor could it make payments on its debts to its bondholders. Under the Code of 1937, the school district could have gone into bankruptcy and the bondholders would have been forced to line up with all other creditors to receive any payment. Furthermore, 51 percent of its creditors would have to approve a plan of reorganization under Chapter 9 of the Act. And once the move into Chapter 9 occurred, revenues normally dedicated to the payment of bondholders could have been allocated for any purpose, thereby converting bondholders into general creditors. However, the school district chose to avoid the stigma of repudiation of its debts because this would have impaired its future ability to borrow. It was able to do so because amendments to the Bankruptcy Code in 1988 secured the interests of the bondholders even though the school district went into bankruptcy. Under the amended Code, the creditors could not put the municipality or school district into bankruptcy involuntarily, despite financial mismanagement, in contrast to corporate bankruptcy. The distinction is significant because it was recognition of the sovereignty of the public entity, once again contradicting the conventional wisdom's claim of no difference in bargaining between the two sectors. Although the bankruptcy of the public body must be voluntary, neither the municipality nor the school district can proceed without the authorization of the state government.

In the San Jose case, a bankruptcy plan was agreed upon under the amended Bankruptcy Code administered by a federal court. While the agreement secured the claims of the bondholders, the school district challenged its obligations to pay its nonbonded debts, in particular the wage claims of its organized schoolteachers. Under the plan applicable to nonbonded debts, the court ruled that the San Jose School District could reject the bargaining agreements it had previously signed with its teachers and other employees, *and even roll back wages!* Later, however, the school district resolved its dispute with the teachers and other employees with an agreement to fund about 60 percent of the promised increases.

3. The Philadelphia Story, 1992[4]

Philadelphia illustrates the third model of municipal response to bankruptcy or, in this instance, the imminent threat of bankruptcy, associated with municipal unionism and collective bargaining. Unlike the other two models, the effective leadership of a newly elected mayor, Edward Rendell, staved off insolvency without surrendering sovereignty to an administrative board or court. Particularly noteworthy is how Rendell addressed not only the typical labor relations problems associated with collective bargaining, but also how management dealt with the City's numerous vendors of goods and services in order to restore fiscal solvency.

When Mayor Edward Rendell took office on January 6, 1992, the City of Philadelphia was on the verge of financial collapse. It was running a $230 million deficit on a $2.3 billion a year operating budget. On his fourth day as mayor, the City was so low in funds that it was preparing to skip a payroll; this was only averted after the City requested and received the approval of a judge that allowed Philadelphia to stretch out payments due to the Employee Pension Fund. The bond rating of the City had fallen to junk bond status. The City had gone into the credit market in November of 1991, a couple of months before Rendell was sworn in, to try to borrow money on short-term notes (the same practice several New York mayors had adopted), but Wall Street would not buy the paper. A group of Philadelphia banks finally loaned the City money at this point for a six-month period, but at a rate of 21 percent in interest and fees. Because of Mayor Rendell's leadership, less than one year later the City was able to borrow the same amount of money, for the same period of time, at a rate of about 4.6 percent.

What can only be described as "textbook" examples of runaway municipal labor costs, excessive compensation, and work rules—Luddism to an advanced degree—were largely responsible for the City's financial situation. The average employee cost the City of Philadelphia more than $50,000 a year in salary and benefits; the City paid 55 cents in benefits for every dollar of wages, well above the average in the private economy. Union work rules were as burdensome as they were outlandish. A joke, which was not apocryphal but an actual fact, recounted that it took three City workers to change a lightbulb at the Philadelphia airport—a mechanic, an electrician, and a custodian!

After months of fruitless talks with the unions for concessions, Mayor Rendell gave the unions a deadline to accept his final offer, which required changes in work rules. He also demanded a cut in paid sick leave from twenty days to twelve and a two-year wage freeze. The unions threatened to strike, and to emphasize their seriousness, they placed full-page ads in newspapers showing piles of uncollected garbage. When the day of reckoning came and some unions did strike, Mayor Rendell's steadfastness and educating the public on the state of affairs—the work rules and excessive labor costs—paid off; he won millions in concessions from the municipal unions after a strike that lasted only sixteen hours.

Meanwhile, Mayor Rendell rejected raising taxes, often a popular but counterproductive program. (In contrast, in 2003, Mayor Bloomberg of New York City has done exactly that, and history awaits the outcome.) With a diminishing tax base, raising taxes would only have further induced individuals and businesses to leave the City. In the eleven years prior to 1992, Philadelphia had raised taxes *nineteen* times. And these were not minor fees or minuscule taxes. They ran the gamut of increases in business taxes, wage taxes, property taxes, and sales taxes. During those nineteen years of increased taxation, 16 percent of the sales tax base left the City. According to a Wharton School study, the City's wage tax alone in those eleven years had cost 150,000 jobs. In fact, the tax burden had become the third highest in the United States, behind only Portland, Oregon, and Milwaukee, Wisconsin.

Rendell also rejected across-the-board layoffs in every department as a means of cutting costs. Instead, he cut the cost of governance across the board. On health costs, the City saved more than $300 million over a four-year period. The average monthly cost per capita for health care associated with the City's four largest unions was about $500. That sum was reduced to about $360 per employee per month. And the new health care plan provided free services, no co-payments, and compared favorably to the best HMO managed care coverage in the City of Philadelphia. Prescriptions were virtually free, requiring only a $1 or $2 co-payment. The dental and optical plans had no co-payments.

Paid holidays were another benefit that had climbed to atmospheric heights. When Rendell became mayor, City workers had about a month and a half of paid days off—a total of forty-seven days per year. These consisted of two weeks paid vacation (ten working days), twenty sick days, and fourteen paid holidays, including both Presidents' Day and Lincoln's Birthday, Election Day, Flag Day, Good Friday, and three administrative leave days that any employee could take at will in order to enable Jewish employees to have the three major Jewish holidays off. To these were added the City's funeral leave policy, which allowed three days off for the death of one of five major relatives in a family. Rendell cut the number of paid holidays from fourteen to ten, a modest beginning.

By increasing the number of work days, the workers not only returned more working time, but ipso facto also reduced the time for which overtime and other penalty rates of pay would be required. For public safety, about 40 percent of the City's workforce—police, firefighters, prison guards, and water service employees—must work holidays, so the reduction in the number of paid holidays also meant a reduction in the number of days requiring overtime pay for security workers. Hence, on Flag Day, or on any other negotiated holiday, every essential worker would be paid at overtime rates; the elimination of frivolous paid holidays saved millions in overtime on each holiday converted to a work day.

Rendell also improved the disability system, which, like the holiday and other benefits, was out of control. Under the prevailing system a worker could get a partial pension and workmen's compensation at the same time. In fact, the disability system paid workers more for not working than it did for working. Not surprisingly, there were frequent examples of double dipping. Like the lightbulb example in the airport, there was an egregious disability case revealed by the *Philadelphia Inquirer.* A worker claimed that he was injured at work when he slipped on some catsup at a seafood restaurant while at lunch; he claimed the injury was a work-related disability because he was lunching with two other employees of his department and they were discussing business matters. He wound up getting an award from the Pension Board of well over $1 million.

Mayor Rendell also addressed the high labor costs of other governmental or quasi-governmental bodies like the school districts, reducing their benefit packages by over $400 million. He negotiated a new contract with the nonuniformed municipal unions, and won arbitration awards with police and firefighters' unions that produced millions in concessions over a four-year period. The mayor admitted, nevertheless, that the City probably had not done all that it could have. At the end of Rendell's first fiscal year, he had eliminated a $450 million deficit without raising taxes. Despite the magnitude of these cost savings and the threats of striking, Mayor Rendell said that implementing his program with the unions was relatively easy.

To deal with these and other exorbitant benefits and to balance the budget, Rendell sold city-run nursing services and home and health center services to private operators, and as part of the paring-down process the City planned to privatize another ten services. The mayor also closed a library and reduced hours at others. He replaced 600 traffic lights with lower-cost stop signs. Working closely with the City Council, Mayor Rendell put together a five-year fiscal plan, fulfilling an election campaign promise.

At the same time, Rendell was pivotal in getting the city's $250 million Avenue of the Arts complex under construction by securing $20 million from local philanthropist Walter Annenberg and a $60.6 million grant from the State of Pennsylvania. That project, a complex of theaters and concert halls, along with a $500 million convention center, gave Philadelphia a much-needed economic and cultural boost.

For these and other achievements, Mayor Rendell's union critics claimed that he lacked a vision for the city beyond austerity: "There is a serious problem in a city when the primary concern is just the bottom line," said Thomas Paine Cronin, president of the American Federation of State, County, and Municipal Employees, District Council 47, which represents most of the city's white collar employees. This amazing criticism shows how extensively Luddism permeates municipal unionism. It also parallels the attitudes that the municipal unions in New York City expressed following the Financial Control Board's decision to block Mayor Dinkins's efforts to finance expenditures with long-term debt.

In one move reminiscent of New York's procedures, Philadelphia won some financial breathing room when the State of Pennsylvania's fiscal oversight board, the Pennsylvania Intergovernmental Cooperation Authority, sold $475 million in bonds for the City. The Authority is the chief watchdog over the City's adherence to its five-year plan for fiscal integrity. Under certain conditions it can withhold funding. Although reminiscent of the New York arrangements, this fell short of the degree of New York State's invasion of the City's sovereignty.

Mayor Rendell was not only criticized by local union leaders for his handling of Philadelphia's fiscal crisis; virtually every leader of every national union in the country attacked him. They warned the mayor that he could "run aground on this issue" (rationalizing costs) and threatened that, as a Democrat, he could not count on their political help in the future. (Parenthetically, Rendell was elected easily to the governorship of Pennsylvania in 2002.) The municipal unions weighed in with television ads against privatization plans of the mayor, claiming people would lose their jobs, with fathers coming home unable to feed their families anymore. Like welfare recipients, the municipal unions were claiming a *right* to an income. They also charged that Rendell's program of privatization applied only to blue collar jobs. In fact, Rendell privatized as many white collar services as blue collar services in the first twenty-one months of his mayoralty.

Race was also used to attack Rendell: Unabashed racial appeals were made characterizing the mayor and his advisors as a bunch of white guys in suits who wanted to abolish jobs and benefits from poor hardworking black workers. However, the mayor successfully insulated himself from the worst of these calumnies because of his political alliance with the leading black political figure of Philadelphia, City Council president John Street. The threats and slander did not deter Mayor Rendell from carrying on with his fiscal plans.

The mayor and everyone appointed to a management position took a cut in pay of 5 percent. Mayor Rendell also addressed the cost of goods and services sold to the City by vendors, with the goal of saving more than half the money needed to avoid bankruptcy. He described this part of his reorganization program as management productivity. To that end, he created an Office of Management and Productivity, a first for the City of Philadelphia. Even more effective was the mayor's Private Sector Task Force on Management and Productivity. Under this program, 300 executives were loaned to the City by private businesses who worked full or part time to provide support and recommendations to improve the efficiency of City departments.

In dealing with vendors, the City declared that it would expect at least a 5 percent reduction in the cost of doing business with all vendors who sold to the City without competitive bids. Law firms who did business for the City of Philadelphia were required to cap their fees in advance. The City substituted other law firms for those that refused. The City stopped paying investment bankers for placing bond sales. Instead, their earnings would have to be derived from the sale of the bond issues.

The mayor commented that vendors of a major city have a tendency, either intentionally or unintentionally, to look upon the City as a fatted calf because most of the bureaucrats who deal with them do not care about the costs of the transactions—an attitude obviously shared by municipal unions. Fundamentally, the relationship between vendors and the City government is often a relationship between a political contributor and a candidate, and vendors believe that the candidate will not do anything detrimental to his or her political interests. As with its labor contracts, there was a lack of oversight of vendor contracts by the City. The Rendell administration made it policy to review every vendor contract and, because of this, claimed to have saved millions of dollars.

An egregious example of the absence of oversight in contracts with vendors was a rental lease on office space brought to light by the City's Office of Management and Productivity early in Mayor Rendell's administration. The City had a year-to-year lease in what was classified as a Grade C building in which the Department of Public Welfare was headquartered. The lease on the building included a rental escalator every year of 9 percent. At the time renewal came due early in the Rendell Administration, the City was paying a rental charge of $32 per square foot, compared to $27 per square foot charged by the One Liberty building, the tallest and newest building with the most dramatic architecture in the City of Philadelphia. The City then advised the landlord that unless he renegotiated the lease, the City would leave. The landlord agreed to a renegotiated lease for $8 a square foot! The City proceeded to renegotiate every lease it had and renegotiated them downward, with one exception.

Another vendor service the City addressed was insurance covering City businesses. For example, the Philadelphia Parking Authority, which operates garages and parking lots, requires large coverage of property and casualty insurance and workmen's compensation. In the past, the mayor's favored broker first won the contract for coverage, and then sought a national insurance company to write the insurance. Whatever rate the insurance company charged was then paid by the city. Under Rendell, brokers were required to submit competitive bids for the insurance. Moreover, the same company that won the insurance contract was also required to handle the City's claims.

As a vendor itself, the City had rationalized its charges to some local suburban communities to which it had supplied wastewater treatment services. The year before Rendell became mayor, the City had increased its rates to these communities. One refused to pay the increase and sued to prevent its implementation. Rendell and the Water Department decided to shut off the wastewater service to that town, but under Federal regulations, it had to give the community five years' notice. Philadelphia then warned the town that it was giving notice immediately. Three months later that town settled and paid its water bill.

Instead of resorting to tax increases, Rendell instituted an improved method of collecting revenue, which brought in more tax receipts. In its first year, the City collected about $42 million more from the same tax base. New software enabled the Revenue Department to increase its receipts. The City also started taxing firms and people who had never paid taxes before in Philadelphia. Lawyers and doctors who maintained offices outside the City, but who routinely came into Philadelphia in order to practice, paid no taxes. A doctor who came into one of the City's renowned eye hospitals twice weekly for forty weeks a year to perform cataract operations earned an estimated $2.2 million of income for those eighty days in Philadelphia and did not pay any taxes; now he and others like him do. Similarly, the City was able to tax accountants, lawyers, visiting athletes, and even a plumber, all of whom came to the City to earn income.

Rendell's methods of increasing productivity included such obvious measures as double zip coding the City's mail. In a similar vein, the City lacked an effective way of recovering reimbursement from the State for noncity residents who received treatment at its health center without disclosing their health coverage. Many claimed to be covered by Medicaid, but after the City submitted some patients' bills to the State for reimbursement under the Medicaid program, reimbursement was denied. Or conversely, some disclaimed coverage under Medicaid, although the centers suspected that, given the patients' income profile, they were eligible for coverage by Medicaid. After negotiations with the State of Pennsylvania, the State provided the City with the necessary computerized information on those covered under Medicaid, so the City now knows who is covered before providing treatment at its health centers. This enabled the City to recoup between $12 and $15 million in a year in health costs.

Because of civil service and union rules, incentives to do the job efficiently had dissipated. In an effort to restore incentives, the City established a productivity bank. The City set aside $20 million from which Departments could borrow for items deemed necessary to improve productivity, but which their regular budgets did not cover. A loan committee must first approve the loan. Approval limits the loan to five years, and the department applying for the loan must demonstrate that it can save double the amount borrowed and repay the loan from its budget during the allotted period and with interest. An example of how this worked was the experience of the City's Revenue Department. It borrowed $5.8 million for a new package of software, which in a year was expected to net $9 million in increased collections. Another example was the Streets Department, which borrowed $350,000 for energy-efficient lamps in buildings and within one year was expected to save about $740,000. The Streets Department also borrowed for a computer system to allow it to deploy its sanitation trucks more efficiently; the system cost about $800,000 and was expected to save $4 million in the reduction of overtime and elimination of some middle manager jobs. Mayor Rendell's approach can be distinguished from some mayors of other troubled cities by his willingness to break the traditional limits of governance with new and more efficient ways of delivering services. His approach also sets the Philadelphia "story" apart from New York City's experience.

Education, the Teachers' Unions, and the Living Wage

The most challenging problem for the compatibility of local collective bargaining and municipal governance is public education. Public education is the largest consumer of local public funds and involves the largest union in the country, the National Education Association (NEA). The NEA, which is unaffiliated with the AFL-CIO, has approximately 2.5 million members, and the American Federation of Teachers (AFT) has about 1 million members (AFL-CIO). Both are significant obstacles to improving public education. The reason is simple—they exercise monopoly power. Like any monopoly they vigorously oppose any competitive challenge, such as privatization and/or choice for parents in selecting schools for their children with vouchers, charter schools, or otherwise. The AFT demonstrated that opposition to the most ambitious effort yet to grapple with the failed school system of the City of Philadelphia.

Like the City itself, the Philadelphia school system, seventh largest in the country, was experiencing a huge budget deficit; its problems included low test scores, chronic teacher shortages, and crumbling buildings. The State intervened in 1998 when it enacted a law allowing for a state takeover of the Philadelphia system if it failed to meet certain budgetary and educational goals. When the goals were not reached, by agreement with the City administration, the State proposed an ambitious reform effort that called for turning over dozens of low-performing schools to a private company, the New York–based Edison Schools, Inc., the nation's largest for-profit education company. State officials proposed a contract with Edison believed to be worth more than $100 million. Under the State's plan, Edison would run dozens of schools and consult the central management of the school system. A five-member School Reform Commission established by the takeover plan was to replace the school board. Unsurprisingly, the plan generated fierce opposition from Philadelphia teachers, blue collar school workers, minority leaders, student activists, the school board, City Council, and parent and community groups. About two dozen protesters occupied a school administration building.

School takeovers and school privatization are not new. Forty districts in eighteen states have been taken over, and some places tried private management of individual schools, among them Baltimore, Minneapolis, and Hartford. But Philadelphia would be the largest school district ever taken over by a state government, as well as the largest experiment in school privatization.

However, Governor Schweiker accepted a scaled-down plan because of opposition from Mayor Street and others. The School Reform Commission voted by 3 to 2 to change the Philadelphia school system for more than one-quarter of the City's schools and thousands of children, effective in September 2002. The Commission members appointed by the governor voted for the plan; the two appointed by Mayor Street voted against. Under the plan, twenty schools were turned over to Edison and twenty-two were turned over to other private companies; the City's three major universities, the University of Pennsylvania, Temple, and Drexel, were to participate in overseeing some of the affected schools; an additional twenty-eight were to be run by parents (Associated Press 2002). These schools would privatize not just some of their services, such as food preparation and cleaning, but academic programs as well; the management of teachers would also be overseen by outside companies.

The rising political power of the teachers' unions is the severest challenge to municipal governance. Efforts to improve public education, like those of New York's Bloomberg administration and the reform movement in Philadelphia, are consistently opposed by the teachers' unions. The NEA and the AFT, which, as noted, are likely to merge in the near future, are already the most effective practitioners of political unionism in the United States. The two teachers' unions maintain more political operatives than either political party, or perhaps both. Together with the increased political activities of the AFL-CIO, they are a major reason for my calling the Democratic Party the de facto Labor Party of the United States. My characterization may be challenged by the political position of James Hoffa, president of the Teamsters, AFL-CIO, and perhaps by a few other union leaders, but this is not fatal to it. (The Teamsters union is the largest in the Federation.) Hoffa has changed his union's automatic endorsement of the Democratic Party, the practice by the AFL-CIO and most of the union movement. Hoffa announced his intentions to support Republicans as well as Democrats whom he regards as pro-union (Ryan 2002). A current issue that has led to this rupture is the Teamsters' support for drilling in Alaska. Drilling would lead to new jobs for its members—and for some other unions as well.

On their road to complete merger, local and state groups of the two teachers' unions coordinate activities in such a way as to be de facto one union. Nationally, the two teachers' unions have set up a joint structure to pursue their agenda, the NEAFT Partnership Joint Council. The Council has outlined issues on which both organizations may work together, such as educational standards, labor–management cooperation, and political activity. The Council and the organizations separately insist on increased union participation in instruction and curricula. As part of the merger, I expect that the new union will be an affiliate of the AFL-CIO. Subsequently, I expect the new affiliate will provide the leadership of the Federation, a position that will shift the central body of organized labor in the United States further to the left, politically.

Another dimension of the rising power of the teachers' unions is their impact on the character of the Labor Movement. The combined ranks of the two unions and other government unions are changing the occupational character of the American Labor Movement from a blue collar movement to a white collar movement, as noted above. Because of the size of the teachers' unions, professional workers will constitute the largest occupational group in union membership for the first time in the history of the American Labor Movement. This will only strengthen their challenge to municipal governance.

A third issue that will challenge municipal governance is the growing demand by unions, radicals, and social reformers that cities enact "living wage laws." The living wage actually applies directly to few, if any, unionized workers. So why do unions join forces with activists to win its enactment by municipal governments? In brief, the living wage is no more than a higher minimum wage, and the same economic analysis applies to it as to the minimum wage. The unions' demands for the living wage are motivated by several reasons, none of which are altruistic—as preached—concern for all workers. Self-interest motivates the unions' advocacy. Wage scales enacted under the living wage, like the minimum wage, are intended to justify subsequent demands for higher wages in collective bargaining agreements in order to restore the wage differentials diminished by legal enactment of a living wage. Another compelling reason for the unions' demands for living and minimum wages is that these laws help to reduce the competition of lower-paid workers for union jobs. If the living wage provisions do affect some unionized workers, it is tantamount to a confession by the unions that they have failed to gain wage increases for the lowest strata of occupations and now turn to local government to provide the higher wage scales. Paradoxically, the unions' campaigns for the living wage will probably boomerang. To the extent that unorganized workers receive benefits— wage or any other job-related benefits by law—their need to join unions for the same benefits via collective bargaining is reduced. In fact, this dynamic has contributed to the decline of private unionism. Although public sector membership continues to be stable, living wage enactments can be expected to diminish the competitive attractiveness of collective bargaining to gain increases in wages. Historically, it is worth noting that the American Federation of Labor (AFL), a predecessor of the contemporary AFL-CIO and the initiator of the modern American Labor movement, regarded governmental programs like minimum wages in this light, and therefore regularly opposed them until the New Deal in the 1930s.

How Public Employees Became Organized

Another unique aspect of the public sector model of bargaining is how public employees became organized. This history provides insight on why municipal unionism is so effective in bargaining. There are four general reasons for the origin and development of the contemporary public union labor movement: employer assistance; self-organization; most important, the transformation of preexisting public employee organizations into unions; and the absorption of some public employees into unions, principally in the private sector.

Public employers' assistance in unionizing might sound like an oxymoron, but it has played a significant role in the rise of public unionism. Unlike private employers, who universally, or nearly so, oppose the unionization of their employees, public employers have often encouraged the unionization of employees under their administration for political reasons. Public employers often dress their motivations in the pious slogans of helping low-paid workers. At times public employers have encouraged unionism and collective bargaining so decisively that, were the same actions taken by a private employer, the labor organization would be ruled company-dominated under the National Labor Relations Act. The National Labor Relations Board would find that these practices violated the right of employees to form, join, and assist labor organizations of their own choice. The Board would declare the employer's relations with the labor organization to be an unfair labor practice and remedy the violation by disestablishing the labor organization. Disestablishment means that the organization can never represent the employees even if it could sever its illegal relationship with the employer.

However, such is not the case in the public domain; the sector is not subject to the NLRA. A preeminent example of employer interference with the right to organize was the unionization of Los Angeles County's 70,000 to 80,000 home care workers in February 1999.[5] Their unionization was hailed by the Service Employees International Union (SEIU), the AFL-CIO, the media, and the County government as a dramatic example of successful unionization of low-paid workers. Even if this were accurate, which it is not, it occurred in the public labor market, not the private market. That is why efforts to organize the home care workers succeeded while the campaign to organize the strawberry workers failed.

The unionization of L.A. County's home care workers began with the enactment of a state law permitting local jurisdictions to create an agency that would become the legal employer of the home care employees. The law was enacted as a special concession to public sector unions, because hitherto they had been unable to organize in the old-fashioned way. Unions lobbied vigorously for the law because prior to its enactment, the union most directly involved, the Service Employees International Union, AFL-CIO, was unable to organize the thousands of Los Angeles County home care workers. Before the enactment of that law, the County employed the home care workers as independent contractors. Under that system, the SEIU, then led by John J. Sweeney (now president of the AFL-CIO), was unsuccessful for more than a decade in organizing home care workers throughout California. To overcome the union's lack of success, the new law enabled L.A. County (and all other jurisdictions in California) to establish a single public employer of its home care workers, replacing previous arrangements under which individuals had contracts with the County.

That enactment facilitated the organization of the home care workers because it created at the same time the unit appropriate both for a representation election and for collective bargaining. Under the new law, in 1997, Los Angeles County proceeded to establish a fifteen-member Personal Assistance Services Council (PASC) and made it the employer of the County's thousands of home care workers. The members of PASC, who serve without compensation, are appointed by the county supervisors. Of these, at least eight were present or past recipients of the County's In-Home Support Services Program (former welfare clients, in other words), while the other members were recruited from among consumer activists. They could also be members of the SEIU; no other "public members" were specified. Only employees of the County were specifically excluded from membership on the Council—hardly a provision avoiding employer assistance and domination of the labor organization.

Neither the County's PASC nor the county supervisors opposed or objected to any of the union's organizational activities. Quite the contrary, each of them encouraged and abetted the union's organizational campaign. Indeed, the chairman of the Los Angeles Board of Supervisors publicly championed the creation of the Council and its operations. Such encouragement of unionization in the private sector had been banned by the implementation of the NLRA. Under these circumstances, if the NLRA applied to the public sector, is there any reasonable doubt that the National Labor Relations Board would have found that (a) the union was the creature of the L.A. County Board of Supervisors, and (b) the County's subsidiary, the Personal Assistance Services Council, actively interfered with the free choice of the home care workers? The make-up of the Council, its control over policy, and the Council's encouragement of the "organizing drive" would, in the private sector, have led the NLRB to find these groups guilty of unfair labor practices for dominating a labor organization and to order the disestablishment of the SEIU's tainted local as the bargaining representative of the home care employees. Under the NLRA, as a result of the Taft–Hartley Act's amendments in 1947, a local of an international union could be disestablished because of a "sweetheart" arrangement establishing the local as the employees' bargaining representative. This episode also casts a revealing light on Sweeney's boastful claims of being a successful organizer. Because of the County's actions, after more than a decade of failure, the Service Employees International Union was able to enroll the County's home care workers. It would be naive to regard the representation election as untrammeled, unaffected by employer preference, yet the union's win of the representation election was greeted with applause by sympathetic media and academics.

The Los Angeles County model was emulated in Oregon in December 2001, when about 13,000 home care workers joined SEIU Local 503 following a mail-ballot election. Oregon made it even easier for its home care workers to vote union than did Los Angeles, where workers had to go to a polling station to cast a ballot. Previously, for four years, the union had tried to organize the Oregon workers without success, paralleling the experience of Los Angeles County. After voters, with the active support of organized labor in Oregon, approved the establishment of a statewide commission to become the employer of the home care workers, again paralleling the L.A. procedure, the home care workers were finally organized. The Los Angeles County experience was obviously the model.

In contrast to the two examples of elections organized and supported by public management, the available record for all representation elections in the public sector shows that representation elections have played a *minor* role in organizing government employees (Juravich and Bronfenbrenner 1998). The data show that over 92,500 state and local employees were reported as "net gains" from these procedures in 1991 and 1992. Yet state and local membership increased by only 32,000 during this period, or less than one-third the "net gains" of employees choosing unions. If coverage instead of membership is used, then state and local union representation actually *fell* by 55,000 (Hirsch and Macpherson 2000, Table 1g, 18). The number of representation elections held in the public sector is small because unions do not need them: as already pointed out, unions are frequently encouraged by public management to organize and bargain, as in the case of Los Angeles County. It is no surprise that when public employees do have a representation election, regularly 80 percent or more vote yes. In contrast, in the private sector, unions win barely 50 percent of such elections. While private management opposes unionization of employees, the outcomes are subject to the procedures of the NLRB and the judiciary in order to determine whether there was illegal employer interference. In contrast to such interference in the private sector, it is a rarity, perhaps even unknown, to find examples of employer interference to prevent unionization in the public sector. In fact, as just detailed above, that interference is typically *in support* of unionism and collective bargaining.

On the other hand, decertification of union representation is virtually unknown in the government domain, while in the private labor market, where the process has existed since 1947, unions lose the overwhelming percentage of referenda. These factors indicate that labor–management relations in the public labor market are frequently less than at arm's length, yet another characteristic making labor–management relations in government unique.

The third method by which public employees became organized was the transformation of existing public employee groups into unions. The two most important examples were the National Education Association, independent of the AFL-CIO, and the American Federation of Teachers, an affiliate of the Federation. Until the 1960s, both regarded themselves as professional associations, not unions. The AFT, even though a longtime affiliate of the American Federation of Labor and then the AFL-CIO, abjured the strike and collective bargaining. But following President Kennedy's Executive Order 10988 issued in 1962, which facilitated unionism and collective negotiations in the federal government, state and local governments adopted policies fostering unionism and bargaining. That in turn led the two major teachers' organizations to transform themselves into unions embracing bargaining and striking, even though strikes were banned almost everywhere by law. Hundreds of other organizations of state and local government employees—public employee associations—and professional associations like the American Association of University Professors likewise transformed themselves into unions and engaged in bargaining as a result of state and local governmental policies favoring unionism and collective bargaining.

The fourth way in which public employees and other groups became unions was their absorption or merger with existing unions, principally those in the private sector. The outstanding example of a private union acquiring public employee groups was the Building Service Employees International Union, an affiliate of the AFL-CIO. In taking this step, the union also transformed itself. It changed from an otherwise small union of building service jobs (of importance in large cities because of its strategic position) into one of the largest unions in the country. Because of the transformation from a private to a predominantly public sector union, it also changed its name to the Service Employees International Union. The conversion was accomplished under the aegis of John J. Sweeney and was doubtless a major factor in his elevation to the office of AFL-CIO president due to the popular belief that he had succeeded in organizing. However, the actual key to his success as president of the Service Employees International Union was not organizing the unorganized, but merger and acquisition, a technique typically associated with financial markets. Many other private sector unions jumped in to pick up organizations and members, because gaining members and organizations was so easy, and because they were losing large numbers of members in the private labor market. None, however, enjoyed the success of Sweeney and the SEIU.

Characteristics of Local Bargaining

The unique character and power of collective bargaining in the public sector stems in part from the history of labor relations in government prior to collective bargaining. Like the contemporary public employee unions, their predecessor organizations, public employee and professional associations, relied on lobbying and political actions to gain improvements in earnings and working conditions. That experience lay the groundwork for the present system of collective bargaining and, again, is most clear-cut and most far-reaching among municipalities and school boards.

As in the private sector, governmental labor relations are local, but localism in collective bargaining enhances the key difference between the two sectors because of its *political dimension*. Localism in governmental collective bargaining is embedded in the structure of both the unions and government. Overall, there are an estimated 45,000 local and district unions in the Labor Movement. Approximately 44 percent may be in the public sector, based on the proportion of total membership in government employee unions. The number of local governmental jurisdictions is also very large, over 87,000, so, like the unions, the structure of the political jurisdiction is a priori set up to bargain at the local level. The number of full-time equivalent employees at the state and local level was about 15 million in 2002.

Although the participants are structurally similar, the "public employer" is unique because it is a sovereign authority negotiating on behalf of a client, the taxpayer. The cost of the negotiations are borne by the taxpayer and the concept of sovereignty is damaged as well. Collective bargaining, ipso facto, implies a diminution and a sharing of sovereign authority, and a shifting of the financial burden to a diffuse group, among which the individuals may not perceive the costs they must bear. These consequences become evident in how municipalities are governed, how public education is delivered, and why unit labor costs can become so steep as to lead to bankruptcies of both school boards and municipalities. Although bankruptcies occur and are far more frequent in the private sector, the fact that a public jurisdiction can be bankrupted cannot be equated with the profit/loss risk in the private sector.

The conventional wisdom views the power sharing through collective bargaining in the public sector as equivalent to the diminution of managerial prerogatives in the private sector. Not only is this analogy simplistic, it obscures the underlying and radical changes that affect public governance. Power sharing also contrasts with the adversarial relationship between representatives of the workers and management in the private sector. There have been periodic demands, mostly from academics (Kochan, Katz, and McKersie 1986), to introduce power sharing into the private sector beyond collective bargaining as well, using not the model of the public sector, but the German model of co-determination. Not surprisingly, private employers have ignored or resisted these demands, realizing the extent to which their ability to manage the enterprise would be circumscribed. Public management has, in contrast, frequently accepted the concept and practice of co-determination.

The key to public management's acceptance of power sharing or co-determination is once again traceable to the political dimension of collective bargaining in the public sector. Public employers or managers are also politicians who are dependent on the support of their bargaining "adversaries" at election time to help retain their public positions. This poses a conflict of interest between their role as employers and managers, and their role as public officials functioning on behalf of the electorate, especially those who pay taxes. Dependence upon the electoral support of their "partners" in collective bargaining—the unions—who are also their political supporters, diminishes their ability and willingness to resist extravagant demands.

The political support that unions give to their employer bargaining

"opponents" spells out the conflict of interest between the public officials' bargaining responsibilities and their political interests. Unions'
political support of favored candidates and platforms comes in two forms,
cash and in-kind (Troy 2000a). Of the two, the latter is far more important, especially in municipal and school elections. While the cash contributions are very significant, I contend that the in-kind form exceeds
them. There are three major sources of in-kind unions support: (1) manpower; (2) dissemination of information; and (3) organizational, based
on the union structure. Manpower, or free labor time, comes from two
sources—union members and employees of unions. Both provide electioneering services of all types without charge to a candidate or the political party endorsed by the union. The difference is that employees of
unions are given time off with pay to work for the unions' endorsed
candidates and party, while members work at no charge, or at least that
is what is widely believed. The total number of individuals drawn from
both sources is not known, although unions have said they can be counted
in the "thousands." No one knows how many persons unions employ,
including the Labor Department.

The second type of support, informational support, consists of the
unions' websites, e-mail, and newspapers and magazines. These uniformly endorse the bureaucracies' favored candidates and political party
(the Democratic Party) and are sent to over 16 million members nationally, implying an audience of some 32 million. The publications carry
the union's recommendations of candidates and political party, and dis-
regard or denigrate those of the political opposition; all union media are
paid for by members' dues and fees from nonmembers, both compelled
by union shop or agency shop agreements.

The third type of support, organizational, flows from the structure of
unions in the United States. As already noted, there are an estimated
45,000 unions in the country. Of these, perhaps 44 percent are in the
public sector. District and state organizations are very important among
some governmental unions, notably the American Federation of State,
County, and Municipal Employees, the National Education Association,
and the American Federation of Teachers. The structure itself puts the
unions in a very powerful and influential position to assist candidates
and the political party of choice, particularly at the state and local
levels of government. To the extent that the political axiom "all politics are local" is accurate, the leverage of governmental unions is extremely powerful in municipalities and school districts because these

jurisdictions are the most numerous and the closest to the public employer-politicians. They can help or hurt a great deal.

Concluding Comments on Municipal Unionism and Municipal Governance

Can municipal collective bargaining and municipal governance "cohabit," to use an expression that has emerged from French political experience? On the fiscal side—the sources of funds—municipal governments face debilitating losses in their tax bases and the loss of jobs in the private sector in the long run. On the other hand, the services supplied by municipalities face almost intractable demands stemming from the decline of family units, a dependent welfare population, the need to deal with the widespread use of drugs, crime, a dysfunctional school system, and, of course, municipal unionism. Because collective bargaining is inextricably linked to political logrolling, an efficient reconciliation of governance with municipal unionism is a greater challenge than at any other level of government or in the private sector.

The three models of insolvency discussed here demonstrate the acuteness of the observation that "labor obligations are among the most burdensome problems faced by municipalities" (James Spiotto, quoted in Troy 1994, 154). Reorganization of bankrupt local governmental bodies, whether de facto or de jure, is not the equivalent of the "exit voice" of failed private businesses. Markets will substitute new or reorganized businesses for failed businesses, with replacements affording the private consumer alternatives. But public consumers, the citizens, have no alternatives to the same political jurisdiction that failed financially, except to emigrate. Separately and collectively, these factors demonstrate that arguments equating public sector collective bargaining with the private sector kind are wrong. Public sector bargaining, especially at the local level, is sui generis.

Based on the experiences of the three models examined above, I conclude that unions can be compatible with municipal government, but at the price of high labor costs; deficiencies in the quality of service, especially in education; the threat and occasional reality of insolvency; and an elision of democratic governance. However, the public seldom understands that price. When insolvency has occurred, its consequences were obviated by a higher level of government (the State, in the case of New York City), or another branch of government (the San Jose case).

Neither of these alternatives was invoked in Philadelphia because the mayor confronted the problems and overcame them, at least during his term of office. Perhaps only when municipal insolvency is resolved by de facto bankruptcy will the public recognize the tension between policies promoting municipal collective bargaining and municipal governance. As cities suffered financial strains, defenders of public sector unions spoke of "ungovernable cities" (Cannato 2001), a political excuse for the' failures of municipal management. I believe that allowing cities to go bankrupt may be the restorative necessary to sound municipal governance. Perhaps only then will the sources of funds (taxpayers) and users (demanders) of municipal funds learn that municipalities do have limited resources. Bankruptcy is the surrogate for competition in the private economy; bankruptcy could introduce the discipline that private labor relations confront, but which is absent in public labor relations. The prevailing attitude in the public sector recalls the cynicism of King Louis XIV of France, whose profligacy led him to declare, "*Apres moi, le deluge.*"

The Philadelphia story shows that municipalities are manageable, contrary to what some have claimed. However, that success depended on one man. Institutionally, the existing arrangements remain. Unlike the private sector, where domestic and international markets (competition) check the monopoly power of unions, in the public sector, countervailing forces are limited: privatization and contracting out are the two most often involved, but they are limited by the unions' political power. Hence, the compatibility of municipal unionism and bargaining with municipal governance will lurch from one episode to another.

Finally, I not only believe that a promising area of research lies ahead in the subject of municipal unionism and municipal governance, but that this research has been ignored due to the conventional wisdom's erroneous claim that bargaining in the public sector is merely an extension of that in the private labor market. If this chapter dispels that notion, it will have made a contribution to answering its central question: "Are Municipal Collective Bargaining and Municipal Governance Compatible?"

Origins of the Brave New World

White collar unionism and the New Unionism do not share a common origin. Instead, the origins of each differ according to the labor market sector in which they are embedded. In the public labor market, governmental pro-union policies, coupled with the absence of competition in furnishing services, generated the phenomenal growth of white collar unionism. President Kennedy's Executive Order 10988 in 1962 inaugurated the growth of union membership at all levels of government by initiating the organization of federal employees, most of whom held white collar jobs. Kennedy's policy was emulated by public officials in many state and local jurisdictions, often with even more vigorous encouragement of their employees to join unions. By about 1994, unions may have reached the saturation point in the public domain; certainly, membership and density stabilized at that time (Hirsch and Macpherson 2003, Figure 2, 10; Table 1f, 16). This condition parallels the experience of the Old Unionism shortly after World War II. However, while the Old Unionism subsequently began its descent into the twilight zone, no similar experience lies ahead, at least immediately, for the New Unionism.

In the private labor market, the pro-union labor policies of the National Labor Relations Act abetted the development of white collar unionism, but to a considerable extent market competition neutralized the law. Under the Act, white collar employees, including professional employees, have had the same rights to organize and bargain as all other employees covered by the Act since 1935. The Taft–Hartley Act of 1947 actually enhanced the rights of professional occupations to join unions by virtually guaranteeing them separate representation units. This requirement facilitates organizing and bargaining for specialized groups by avoiding their submergence into larger units dominated by manual workers with little knowledge of the professionals' needs and aspirations. Nevertheless, white collar workers subject to the NLRA, before and after Taft–Hartley, have overwhelmingly rejected unionism and collective bargaining.

There are several reasons for the unions' poor performance in the private sector, aside from market factors: Most white collar workers in the private sector have historically been hostile to unionization for occupational reasons, as private polls and NLRB representation elections have shown. The unions themselves have not been attuned to their needs, just as they were not organizationally prepared to organize blue collar workers in manufacturing during the 1920s. Also, because unions have historically been made up predominantly of blue collar workers, their "instincts" and experience directed their organizing mainly toward other blue collar workers. This appeared to change when John J. Sweeney took office as president of the AFL-CIO in October of 1995, announcing that

> we begin today to build a new AFL-CIO that will be a movement of, by and for working Americans . . . to organize every working woman and man who needs a better deal and a new voice . . . that [o]ur commitment is to revitalize the labor movement at every level and to change its face to represent the faces of all American workers. (Bureau of National Affairs 1996)

In addition to the strawberry workers, Sweeney identified white collar workers, especially professional and technical workers, as principal targets. The Federation recognized that the task would not be easy; it acknowledged that the workers of the new millennium have different needs and aspirations from those in the past. The Federation identified employee participation programs and supervisors as obstacles to the unionization of white collar groups. (The NLRB has ruled some employee participation programs to be company-dominated organizations; supervisors are excluded from coverage of the law and are therefore almost impossible to organize.) Despite Sweeney's declarations to launch major organizational campaigns, polls, NLRB representation elections, and membership statistics continue to show that the Old Unionism is waning.

A contradiction of my assessment regarding the impediments to organizing private sector white collar occupations may have occurred with the settlement of the forty-day Boeing strike in March 27, 2000, involving professional engineers. The union of 13,000 members won a contract settlement that met most of its demands (Franklin 2000). This led to the widespread belief that (private) white collar unionism had turned the corner, *even though the strike had nothing to do with the unionization of Boeing engineers.* In fact, Boeing engineers had been organized for many years. Instead of being an organizational strike, the dispute was over the terms and conditions of employment. Despite the true nature of the strike, union leaders and many in the media viewed the outcome as a portent of future inroads among high-tech and white collar workers in the private sector. Similar examples of apparent union successes among white collar employees were the organization of some academics at *public* institutions of higher learning and, in addition, some college and university staff personnel, as well as teaching and graduate assistants, at both public and private institutions. One of the largest single gains reported among teaching assistants was that of the United Auto

Workers at eight campuses of the University of California campuses, a public institution. In general, the union was said to have organized some 30,000 employees of colleges and universities (Meister 2000).

These developments underscore the decline of major private sector unions, rather than representing a major turn in organizing unorganized white collar employees in private institutions. It demonstrates that declining private sector unions are grasping for new members well outside their historic jurisdictions, and that in enrolling teaching and graduate assistants they are also enrolling an unstable membership, individuals who have a high turnover and whose financial contributions to the union are small because of their low incomes. In fact, a major part of their income is in-kind—that is, remission of their fees by the university or college. These new members will likely be financially costly for the unions to service and maintain. Such gains are shaky grounds for rebuilding unions whose core members are highly paid workers, for, historically, unions became permanent institutions by organizing workers whose occupations were stable.

There are other examples of white collar professionals joining unions that have been brought up as evidence of the transformation to white collar unionism. Some medical doctors have joined and formed unions and, indeed, they are a substantive addition to white collar unionism. Several unions from the private and public sectors are making efforts to attract physicians. The Office and Professional Workers International Union, AFL-CIO, has established a separate body within the union, the National Guild of Medical Professions, to provide political support and magnify the voice of these members in health care issues. As yet the Guild is unable to bargain collectively for physicians, though its long-term plan is to do so (Knight 2001). The Guild is said to have 20,000 members, but Gifford's *Directory of U.S. Labor Organizations, 2001* does not report the Guild as an affiliated organization. The American Federation of State, County, and Municipal Employees, AFL-CIO, has established two affiliates of physicians, the Union of American Physicians and Dentists, claiming 6,000 members and ten affiliates, established in 1972, and the Federation of Physicians and Dentists, claiming 8,500 members. The former is listed in the *Directory of U.S. Labor Organizations, 2001*, but the latter is not. The American Medical Association (AMA) set up an organization known as Physicians for Responsible Negotiations (it is not listed in the *Directory of U.S. Labor Organizations, 2001*). The AMA requires that the organization not strike. The "no strike" policy was the original position of the two major teachers' organizations (as noted above), but was later abandoned; perhaps this will be the future path taken by the AMA's Physicians for Responsible Negotiations.

At least five states and the District of Columbia have proposed legislation that would encourage collective bargaining by physicians. In 1999, the National Labor Relations Board added to the stimulus of transforming the Labor Movement by reversing an earlier ruling when it decided that interns, residents, and fellows have the right to organize (NLRB 1999, 330). Whether this ruling by a Clinton-dominated labor board will survive a Bush majority remains to be seen. Also, a judicial ruling may test it. The rise and expansion of health maintenance organizations is probably a major reason for the beginnings of collective bargaining by physicians. At this point, however, it is premature to forecast a major surge of unionization and collective bargaining by physicians in the process of transforming the Labor Movement.

Among other health care professionals, large numbers of nurses have been represented and have bargained for many years; most are apparently in the public sector and therefore already a part of the transformation of the Labor Movement. However, in the private sector, a recent Supreme Court decision decided that nurses classified as supervisors are not covered by the National Labor Relations Act, a ruling that reversed a previous National Labor Relations Board decision. Until then, nurses, even though classified as supervisors, were eligible to join unions (Labor Research Association 2001). The decision is a setback to unions because it will make it more difficult to organize nurses in the private sector. It also reinforces the public nature of the transformation of organized labor. Unions and their academic supporters have long sought to change the definition of supervisor and thereby change their coverage under the National Labor Relations Act, ever since the Taft–Hartley Act of 1947 exempted supervisors from coverage under the law.

Because of projected occupational trends in the new millennium, the unions' problems in organizing white collar workers in the private sector will become even more difficult. The Labor Department's estimates of projected employment, 1998–2008, indicate almost all of the expected job growth will be in the private service industries; professional jobs will lead the list in occupational expansion and most will be in the private labor market (U.S. Bureau of Labor Statistics 2001), where densities are low. The same categories of employment led in the expansion of white collar jobs over the 1988–98 period. Given the past failure of unions to organize these occupations in the private economy, there is no reason to expect that they will be able to reverse the pattern in the years ahead; in fact, the probability is that density will fall even further.

Internationally, the American white collar union movement lags behind all other G-7 countries. The explanation for the lag is that public policy in those nations has encouraged unionism among white collar employees in the public sector sooner and to a greater extent than has U.S. policy. Consequently, in the transformation from the blue to white collar unionism, the American Labor Movement, while "catching up" with white collar unionism in all other G-7 countries, will also continue to lag. In fact, as just pointed out above, the New Unionism has probably encountered stagnation.

The process of organizing as well as the development of unionism in the two labor markets has also been different; it also accounts for the much more successful unionization of white collar occupations in the public compared to the private labor market. In the public domain, the organization of government workers has been largely the result of "organizing the organized," and mergers and acquisitions. By the term "organizing the organized," I mean the transformation of existing professional and public employee associations into unions. The leading example of such a transformation, as mentioned before, is the National Education Association. The NEA dates from 1857 and historically distinguished itself as a professional association; traditionally it opposed unions and collective bargaining. However, after the new federal, state, and local policies promoting public employee unionism and bargaining in the 1960s, the NEA faced a challenge from the American Federation of Teachers (AFT), an affiliate of the AFL-CIO, to represent teachers in major cities across the country. In order to meet the challenge, the NEA transformed itself into a union and began to engage in representation elections, collective bargaining, and strikes. (Incidentally, the AFT, although an affiliate of the American Federation of Labor since the early years of the twentieth century and later of the AFL-CIO, had also historically proclaimed its professional character and avoided bargaining and strikes until the revolution in public policy toward unionism beginning in the early 1960s.)

Supplementing the process of "organizing the organized" was the process of mergers and acquisitions of many independent public employee organizations with established unions. Many public employee associations faced a Hobson's choice: compete as independent unions or merge with established unions. One private organization that benefited significantly from the dilemma of the independent public employee associations was the Service Employees International Union. One of its greatest successes in acquiring a public employee organization was its absorption of a California public employee association; this, in a single stroke, added perhaps 100,000 to its membership.

Academic supporters of organized labor are suggesting that the conversion of associations into unions in the public sector could be a model for extending unionism to professionals in the private sector (Hurd 2000). There are professional associations in the private sector (their number and membership is not known), and if these could be transformed into unions, the changeover would mark a major step in the unionization of private professional groups. It would be a development far outweighing the unions' prospects of organizing the unorganized. However, the comparability to the experience of the public sector is limited, and the prospects of similar transformations from associations to unions in the private sector are also limited.

Before becoming unions, the public sector associations had a great deal of experience in lobbying their public employers, and although not the equivalent of collective bargaining, the practices were similar, so after conversion to unionism these associations were prepared to bargain. It is true, of course, that private sector associations also lobby governments to establish and protect their professional standards, so there is an analogy to a degree. However, unlike public associations, private professional associations will not receive the encouragement of their private employers to become unions, as did the public employee associations. Those who believe that private professional and technical associations will become unions postulate that "de-professionalization" of their occupations (downgrading of their skills) could provide the rationale for the transformation to unionism (Hurd 2000, 26–27). However, such a negative trend in professionalism seems unlikely given the pace of scientific and technological advance that lies ahead in the new century. Meanwhile, Hurd concedes:

> [W]orkers who view professional associations as preferable to other organization forms [i.e., unions] seem to think of themselves as *individual* professionals. They are relatively more satisfied with their work, interested in exercising discretion on the job, and attracted to professional development to enhance their own skills. They are concerned

that unions might create conflict or at least increase tension and thus have a negative influence on the work environment. (Hurd 2000, 18, emphasis in original)

In my judgment, if private sector professionals are to become union members to any significant extent, unions will have to rely on the old-fashioned way of organizing—"organizing the unorganized," or the "bottom-up" approach—a procedure that has enjoyed little success to date. Organizing the unorganized in the public sector is of little importance, or more accurately unnecessary, because unions and employees are often encouraged by public management to organize and bargain.

In addition to differences in how workers get organized in the two sectors, the growth of employment among white collar occupations has also had contrasting effects on unionism in the public and private sectors. In the public labor market, gains in employment almost automatically translate into gains in representation and to some degree in membership as well. In contrast, gains in white collar jobs in the private sector rarely increase membership, but also usually cause a reduction in density.

The difficulties in organizing white collar workers are not unique to the United States. In Britain, white collar unionism is greater in density than in the United States, but has stagnated despite the pro-union policies of the governing Labour Party. Although unionized white collar workers in Britain now account for a slightly larger proportion of total membership than do blue collar workers (*Daily Mail* 2000, 15), the reason is the severe decline in blue collar membership, rather than the growth of white collar membership. From 1979 to the mid-1990s, British unions lost 5 million members, a loss proportionately larger than the U.S. loss for the equivalent period. British union membership dropped from 12 to 7 million and most of these membership losses were among blue collar workers, just as in the United States. The shrinkage, combined with the stability of white collar members in the public sector and perhaps modest gains in the private sector, shifted the overall balance of union membership from blue to white collar, mirroring the process unfolding in the United States. To promote white collar unionism in the private sector, the Blair government adopted regulations encouraging employees' rights to trade union representation and recognition. It has been claimed that the new regulations *could* result in an increase of up to 2 million new members. The gains are expected to be made up primarily of women and professional, skilled, white collar employees. Whether these expectations will be fulfilled remains to be seen.

Philosophy, Policies, and Consequences of the Brave New World

What the transformed organized labor movement will do in its "Brave New World" will basically be determined by the philosophy and policies of the unions in the public sector and, in particular, by the teachers' unions (Troy 1999). Numerically, the teachers' unions are the largest and may even rival police and firefighters as the most organized occupational group in the Labor Movement. The combined membership of the two teachers' unions is currently about 3.5 million, or about 20 percent of the total U.S. union membership and over 40 percent of all members in the New Unionism. In time, the teachers will surely become the power center within the AFL-CIO, a development that will follow the merger of the two teachers' unions and the affiliation of the new union with the Federation. Their orientation is to the political left, a position already shared with the leadership of the AFL-CIO, so the new combination will reinforce that political stance. As previously stated, the essence of the philosophy of the teachers' unions, and of all public sector unions, is the redistribution of more of the national income from the private to the public economy. While public unionism's demands for higher wages and other terms and conditions of employment *appear* to be the same as the demands of the private unionism, the bargained results differ significantly. While seeking *more* from government employers, public unionism is effectively demanding that an increased share of the national income be transferred to and spent by government: thus, their *micro* demands have *macro* consequences.

It might be argued that the unintended macro consequences of wage demands by private unionism are inflationary wage/price pressures, but that analysis requires acceptance of the theory of wage (cost) push inflation, a theory that depends on the absence of a response by the monetary authorities. Analogously, private sector unionism has a related set of political objectives. Succinctly stated, it embraces a philosophy of neo-mercantilism, a philosophy that demands more government intervention in labor markets, particularly in labor law, on wages (minimum and living wages), and the inclusion of wage and other conditions in future international trade agreements in order to stifle global competition (Troy 1999). The political consequences of the philosophies of redistribution and neomercantilism have already reshaped the political landscape. Al Gore won the Democratic nomination for the presidency in 2000 with the help of the unions, especially the teachers. During the presidential election, organized labor gave major contributions in money and in-kind assistance to Gore and the Democrats. Although Gore lost, the extent of organized labor's help to the Democratic Party in recent years is extremely significant. (This relationship will be assessed in detail in Chapter 6).

Conclusions: The Brave New World

The American Labor Movement has reached a new watershed in its history, one comparable to the founding of the AFL (1886), the CIO (1937), and the rise of the New Unionism (1960s). At the onset of the new century, a plurality, soon to become an absolute majority of organized labor, will wear white collars. And significantly, the majority of these members are and will continue to be employees of government. These new characteristics are transforming the American Labor Movement. However, the transformation is far more than a change in statistical characteristics; the watershed dividing the past from the future constitutes a momentous shift in what unions do and why—the "Brave New World" of the American Labor Movement. In the new century, that Brave New World will be directed not by leaders coming from the blue collar working population, but primarily by *middle-class intellectuals employed by government*—in particular, teachers.

Historically, the private blue collar union movement prided itself on its philosophical outlook of pragmatism generated from its experiences in the private marketplace. It accepted capitalism and sought only to modify it for the benefit of members, according to the original philosophy of "more" of the Old Unionism. It rejected the influence of intellectuals in or outside the Labor Movement. Now, that practice is being reversed. Intellectuals employed by government, whose ideas and philosophy are shaped by an anti-market ideology, will become *the dominating influence in shaping what unions do and why.* Ideologically they advocate an increasing share of the national income for their industry—public employment and especially public education. Serving their ideological objective is a far-reaching organizational structure: several thousand subordinate organizations in every state. The distribution of wealth they seek to effectuate has far-reaching implications not only for state and local governments, but for governance at the national level as well. There is a new kid on the block, and it behooves not just industrial relations specialists and labor economists to take note, but the general public as well.

5

IS THE TWILIGHT OF THE OLD UNIONISM UNIQUE TO THE UNITED STATES?

A Convergence in International Union Trends

Is the Old Unionism's twilight unique to the United States? In a word, no, as comparisons between the United States and the other G-7 countries will demonstrate. The optimal information for the comparative analysis would be trend data that separated the public and private Labor Movements and labor markets across all G-7 countries. However, long-term data on both measures are available only for the United States In all the other G-7 countries, trend information on unions is available for the private and public sectors *combined*, and figures identifying the two sectors are either unavailable or of too recent origin to detail trends. Likewise, employment figures distinguishing between the public and private labor markets comparable to the United States are also unavailable for the other G-7 countries. While the lack of such data for the other G-7 countries is a hindrance to international comparisons, it does not prevent a convincing international analysis (Table 5.1).

The figures in Table 5.1 are of the total of public and private sector membership. Imperfect as they are, the figures indicate that the density of private sector unionism is declining across G-7 countries, because in none are the membership and density of government unionism declining. The cross country declines in density demonstrate that the Old Unionism is subject to the same market forces across all countries. For all, except Canada, Table 5.1 shows that membership has also declined. Total Canadian membership rose only because of the continuing increase of union membership in the public labor market. Beginning in 1997, Statistics Canada introduced a breakdown between the private and public

Table 5.1

Union Membership (M) and Density (D), Selected G-7 Countries, 1980–2002

Year	Canada M 000	Canada D %	Germany M 000	Germany D %	Japan M 000	Japan D %	U.K. M 000	U.K. D %	U.S. M 000	U.S. D %
1980	3,397	37.6	N.A.	N.A.	12,369	30.8	12,947	49.9	20,095	23.0
1990	4,031	35.7	11,800	34.8	12,193	25.2	9,947	38.1	19,075	16.1
2002	4,174	31.1	8,311**	26.1**	11,099*	20.7*	7,550*	29.1*	15,979	13.3

Sources: International Labor Office, Bureau of Statistics, for data that are supplied by individual countries. Additionally, for Canada, Statistics Canada; Japan, Ministry of Health, Labor and Welfare; U.K., Keith Brook Employment Relations Directorate, Department of Trade and Industry, Labor Force Survey; for the United States, Hirsch and Macpherson (2003); Germany, figures for the united country.

Notes: *Denotes figures for 1998; **denotes figures for 2001.

domains, and these data show a decline in density from 21.5 to 19.6 percent of employment, and membership gains of nearly 90,000, indicating that nonunion employment rose more than did union membership. Meanwhile, density of the New Unionism in Canada rose from 71 to 76 percent and membership by almost 400,000 in 1997–2002. However, it is evident that the classification problems that have beset Canadian data continue, and that the officially reported membership gains in the private sector are almost certainly incorrect.

Before examining this issue, I will report on another measure of decline, the Old Unionism across countries—the extinction of many local organizations that are subsidiaries of national bodies. The number of Japanese unions shrank more than 11 percent, from 34,579 in 1984 to 30,773 in 2001 (Table 5.1). The International Labor Office's report for Japan recorded different totals, but also a decline in the number of organizations. From 1980 to 2000, the number of labor organizations dropped from 72,693 to 68,737, a decline of 5 percent (Table 5.1). In the U.K., the number of labor organizations was reduced from 438 to 206, or 53 percent (Table 5.1). German data also reveal a pronounced decline of subordinate organizations (Weiss 2003). Similar official data are not available for Canada. However, I compared the loss of locals in Canada and the United States for the period 1980 to 1985, and found that the number of locals of the same private sector international unions (unions with members and locals in the United States and Canada) had shrunk in both countries. I found that the number of Canadian locals of the same international unions had declined 14 percent compared to 18 percent in the United States (Troy 1990, 133, Table 7). This was further evidence contradicting the spurious claim that Canadian unions had escaped the American "disease." For the United States, the number of unions reporting financial and other information to the Department of Labor declined from about 60,000 in 1959–60, the initial year of registration under the Labor Management Reporting and Disclosure Act of 1959, to about 45,000 in 2002, and that understates the degree of decline because the current number of registrants includes public sector organizations in 2002 that were not required to report in 1959.

Is Canada an Exception in the Decline of the Old Unionism?

The answer is no. This finding is more than a statistical resolution of an academic dispute. It underlies a major policy issue: the demand of union leaders and sympathetic academics who see in the (fallacious) Canadian data justification for importing Canadian labor laws or amending the NLRA to reflect Canadian labor laws. Statistically, the question arises because of the numerous (and again, fallacious) claims of many industrial relations specialists and labor economists that Canadian unionism has escaped the "American disease" of union decline, and that instead it has gained in membership and density over the last several decades. In contrast, I argue that Canadian private sector unionism, the Old Unionism, has indeed declined; that, in fact, the trends in the two countries are converging. By converging I mean that trends in membership and in density are moving in the same direction, a confluence of trends; convergence does not imply a meeting, crossed or parallel in trends, and therefore the word accepts differences in levels of density and membership. Thus, the United States, a much larger country, will have a larger membership numerically; on the other hand, Canada, for numerous reasons, including its much more pro-union labor legislation, federal and provincial, can and does have a higher level of density.

Therefore, the question is, why is there a contradiction about trends, when both models (divergence versus convergence) depend upon common sources of Canadian statistics on unionism and employment? The answer is that while others have accepted official data as given, I have challenged the official data and found that private sector unionism, membership, and density have declined (Troy 2000). Essentially, the reason is that the official Canadian data on membership, density, and employment, for all but the last six years, did not distinguish between private and public sectors with the minor exception of public administration. Beginning in 1997, Statistics Canada introduced for the first time a classification of unionism, employment, and density separating the public from the private sectors of the labor market. However, there are serious problems with these data as with their predecessors, which I shall address later in this chapter.

The most egregious example of the bundling of public and private employees has been in the services sector (which to some extent still applies since the 1997 revisions). The official Canadian data combined public and private services into a single category, in contrast to the United States, where the two are separately identified, with possible minor exceptions. Private employment grew rapidly in this sector in the United States, while in Canada the growth of *services* was, to a very extensive degree, a function of government services. And because the private was combined with public *services* in Canada, the distinction between private and public unionism in this sector and in other sectors, where there was extensive government production, were blurred and yielded misleading results. Thus, health care and education, overwhelmingly public and highly unionized for that reason, were reported simply as *services*, distorting comparisons with services in the United States, where health care is overwhelmingly private and most education is public, and so classified. Thus, unionization in Canadian *services* greatly exceeded that in the United States, and also increased the overall average density of Canadian unionism. The same problems applied to other important Canadian industrial classifications—utilities, trade, mining, and transportation—where public bodies, crown agencies, and crown corporations are or were the employers. And as is the case around the world, including the United States, where public bodies are the employers, unionization of the employees is high and always much higher than in the private labor markets. In brief, then, comparisons of unionism statistics between the United States and Canada were comparisons between "apples and oranges." Yet these false comparisons not only failed to deter the conventional wisdom from making the comparisons, but instead used the results to conclude that Canada's Old Unionism had escaped decline. Moreover, these misleading conclusions were repeated often, like an echo, by scholars around the world.

Beyond specific statistical measures of convergence, several other factors explain why Canada's Old Unionism has not escaped the "American disease." Canada's industrial relations laws, federal and provincial, are patterned after the original Wagner Act, and although they are more pro-union, they have not escaped "repeal" by markets, just like the NLRA. In fact, because these laws are so much more pro-union than the American original, Canadians often refer to them as Super Wagnerism. While Canadian labor laws have *slowed* the decline of the Old Unionism, they not prevented the decline. For policymakers in the United States, the decline of private unionism in Canada, and especially in Quebec, which is itself unique, is a fortiori evidence that an amended National Labor Relations Act favorable to unions will not stem or reverse the Old Unionism's journey to the twilight zone. Incidentally, if the data from Quebec are separated from Canada, then the rest of Canada, especially Ontario, looks more the statistical portrait of the United States. In 2002, Ontario's (official) private sector density was 17.4 percent; eliminating public components in health and education would reduce that rate and bring it even closer to American density.

Another factor affecting the convergence of Canadian and American unionism is the presence of some American unions with locals in Canada, which still account for an important fraction of total Canadian membership.[1] Figures show that these unions have not displayed positive trends north of the 49th parallel and negative trends below it; instead they show similar trends. Some purely Canadian unions, such as the Canadian Auto Workers, report gains in membership, but the gains are not in their core jurisdiction; rather they result from mergers, usually with occupational and industrial groups unrelated to their jurisdiction, including public employees. Not only does this mask the decline in their core jurisdictions, but in a parallel to the general misrepresentation of Canadian trends, such membership gains are hailed as proof of Canadian divergence from American trends. Convergence in trends is fostered by the presence of American companies that are major enterprises in Canada, and to the extent that their policies affect union trends, why should one expect their labor policies to be different in the two countries? Because Canada and the United States are each other's best trading partner, their trading relationship, tariffs, and exchange rates affect trends in the Old Unionism in each country, and they will affect leads and lags in union trends.

Two Models of Canadian Union Trends

Analysts agree that the Canadian and American systems of industrial relations differ—the Canadian being more pro-union—but sharply disagree on the systems' outputs. On both sides of the border the mainstream view is that the two countries' systems have produced major transnational divergences in union trends. According to the mainstream view, private sector union membership and density rose in Canada while declining in the United States over recent decades. Descriptively, the mainstream view is the divergent systems–divergent trends model. My alternative is the divergent systems–convergent trends model. Moreover, my model applies to both the private and public industrial relations systems in both countries: the Old Unionism's membership and density have declined in both countries, while membership and density of the New Unionism have risen in both countries. I treat the private and public systems separately because their histories, attributes, labor organizations, and goals, and, most importantly, the factors governing trends, outweigh the two systems' common characteristics. Union affiliation with a common federation is immaterial. Indeed, sectoral union movements (the Old and the New Unionism) share more transnational than intranational characteristics. Reasons for convergent union decline in the private economies of both countries are those that already have been identified: market forces, including structural changes in labor markets, growing competition in international trade, economic evolution, changes in exchange rates, and deregulation. There is also convergence in the inability of private unions in both countries to offset losses with new organization in their core jurisdictions because of the same market forces. In the public economies of both countries, the size and structure of labor markets and governmental policies are the principal explanatory factors for the growth of the New Unionism.

My divergent systems–convergent trends model found that union density in the Canadian private sector peaked at 34 percent in 1958 and declined thereafter (Troy 1992, Table A-1, 38); that Canadian private density probably lagged the peak in U.S. density by about a decade, after taking account of the Korean War; and that after 1958 it has continued to track the American decline (Troy 1992, Table A-2, 39). Those who have claimed instead that Canadian density began to climb above the American rate relied on the combination of public and private unionism and ignored the distinctions between the two. In the words of a prounion analyst, whose observations have been ignored:

> The upsurge in union membership in Canada in the decade after the mid-1960s, following a period of relative stagnation, if not actual decline, may be attributed almost entirely to the adoption of collective bargaining by government employees at the federal and provincial levels. (Goldenberg 1988)

Because private unionism dominated the average density in the pre-1966 period of decline, Goldenberg's comment identifies *the decline in private sector density.* Goldenberg's comment is also consistent with my conclusion that Canadian private density peaked in 1958. These conclusions, of course, constitute very significant data for my divergent systems–convergent trends model.

Tracking private density in Canada is difficult for the reasons already stated: the absence of trend data. However, for 1990, I had estimated that Canadian private density declined to 18 percent. Nine years later, in 1999, Statistics Canada reported that private density to be 18 percent, and then reported that it rose to 19.6 percent in 2002. These figures are from Statistics Canada's Labour Force Surveys (LFS), which began in 1997 to separate private from public sector union membership and employment. Does this imply that I understated the density of the Old Unionism in Canada in 1990? Perhaps, but since the LFS data continue to include some public with the private sector data, the answer is uncertain.

The continuing problem with Statistics Canada's private sector figures (since 1997) is the agency's inclusion of an unknown number of self-employed individuals classified in the private sector who are actually in the public labor market. Typically, the term *self-employed* implies the private sector, but such is not the case in the Canadian enumeration. Included in the classification are numerous health care providers—doctors, nurses, and technicians—and in Canada the predominant share of these health care providers are part of the country's socialized medicine system. In addition, there are others in education who are also included with the "self-employed" but are paid by government, federal or provincial. Total employment of those classified as self-employed in 2002 numbered about 2.4 million, so their distribution between the private and public labor markets will have a pronounced effect on membership, density, and employment. The significance of the impact is illustrated by an official Statistics Canada commentary on unionization in 2001: "Employees in the public sector—government, crown corporations, and publicly-funded schools or hospitals—were almost four times as likely as their private sector counterparts to belong to a union (70.1% versus 18.4%)" (Statistics Canada 2001, 2).

Clearly, the official Canadian statistics continue to overstate private sector union membership, employment, and density, and understate the public sector figures. Based on the official estimate of 18.4 percent density for private schools and hospitals, I would estimate that the general density for all of the private sector must now be no more than 17 percent, a figure close to the union rate in Ontario, the province most similar to the United States. In part, the Canadian private sector rate is bound to exceed the American because recently privatized public enterprises like Rail Canada, Air Canada, a number of mining companies, and others, continue to have high rates of unionism for a while. After such companies are transferred to the private sector, their density and membership participation change slowly, as experience in Britain has shown. Only after a lapse of time, as private management rationalizes the previously publicly owned companies, would union density decline. By rationalizing, I mean the more rapid substitution of technological changes and employment of more white collar workers, who are less likely to favor unionization.

Other data confirming the decline of the private sector in Canada are the statistics of membership and density in manufacturing, an industrial sector that is predominantly private. As in the United States unionism in manufacturing is the cornerstone of the Old Unionism in Canada. Union density in Canadian manufacturing ebbed from 37.9 percent in 1985 to 29.8 in 2001 (Statistics Canada 2001, Table 1, 4). This marks the lowest unionization rate in manufacturing since the Canadian government began publishing data by industrial sector in 1966. This level of manufacturing density exceeds the American substantially, but differences in levels do not contradict the divergent-convergent trends model. With respect to manufacturing, this is even more the case. While Canada is a larger country than the United States, its amount of territory usable for industrial relocation is far smaller: there is no Sun Belt to move to. Even more important is the diversity of manufacturing in the United States as compared to Canada. As Adam Smith pointed out more than two centuries ago, market size has a huge impact on the specialization of labor, read now specialization of industry. Indeed, California has a larger work force than Canada. So, while nominally appearing to be the same based on titles of industrial classifications, the industries differ in scope and detail. Nevertheless, the conventional wisdom treats industrial titles as though they conveyed identities, much like it treated international comparisons of union membership and density.

My divergent-convergent trends model applies to the New Unionism as well as the Old. In this instance, it explains the *growth* of public unionism in both countries. The growth of public employee unionism has been far greater in Canada for two major reasons: exceptional pro-union public policy and *a relatively larger public sector labor market*, perhaps twice the size of the American (Troy 1990). Logically, this is the necessary condition underlying the extremely high unionization rate of the New Unionism in Canada. The sufficient condition would be the extraordinary pro-union policies of the federal and most provincial governments. In 2002, the New Unionism organized 76 percent of public employment—without doubt, the highest among all G-7 countries. In the United States it is about half that rate, just under 38 percent.

Because of these policies, the New Unionism became the dominant wing of the Canadian Labor Movement between 1975 and 1985; the absence of annual data on private and public unionism precludes the determination of the specific year. To put this amazing development in historical perspective, one must recall that the New Unionism only began its surge to dominance in Canada about a decade earlier and achieved domination within two decades, if not sooner, over a private sector labor movement that dates from the nineteenth century. Until the mid-1960s, the New Unionism was a marginal factor in the Canadian union movement, just as in the United States. The New Unionism is not yet the "senior partner" in the U.S. Labor Movement, but as already noted, I expect it to become the larger of the two wings of organized labor in the near future. This is another consequence of the twilight of the Old Unionism. The take-off of the New Unionism in Canada resulted from Canadian governments, federal and provincial, mimicking the labor policies of the U.S. federal, state, and local governments toward public employee unionism in the 1960s, after President Kennedy's Executive Order, which initiated the rise of the New Unionism. Just like the Canadian emulation of the Wagner Act, mutated into Super Wagnerism, Canadian policies encouraging public employee unionism went well beyond the American original.

The growth of the New Unionism in both countries has led to a shift in the composition of the labor movements of both countries and that marks yet another convergence in trends. Both were once predominantly private labor movements; now the Canadian is predominantly public (as are all the other G-7 countries, except the United States), and, after a lag, the New Unionism in this country will also be the majority. The lag is no more a divergence in trends than is Canada's lag in the decline of private unionism.

Why the Canadian Experience Is Important

The Canadian experience is important to U.S. policy because of its potential justification for new labor law. The AFL-CIO declared nearly two decades ago, and today they would state the same even more forcefully, that

> the Canadian experience . . . is instructive [because] Canada has roughly the same type of economy, many similar employers, and has undergone the same changes [as] the United States. But in Canada . . .

the percentage of the civilian labor force that is organized increased
. . . at the same time the percentage of organized workers declined in
the United States. (AFL-CIO 1985, 15)

The statement relies on the use of the average density to compare the United
States and Canada and is a virtual copy of academic thinking prevalent at
that time, notably the misleading "findings" of Freeman and Medoff (1984).

Employer Opposition

The mainstream identifies employer opposition in the United States as
one of the principal divergences between the Canadian and American
industrial relations systems. The conventional wisdom contends that
employer opposition is more intense in the United States than in Canada
and that this opposition, not structural change, is the primary reason for
the decline of private sector unionism in the United States. This characterization of employer opposition is amazing in view of the admission
that "*Although there is no supporting data, a consensus seems to have
developed that employer resistance to unions in Canada is not as extensive or intense as in the United States*" (Rose and Chaisson 1987, 8,
emphasis added). In other words, why bother about investigating, using
the scientific method, when a "consensus" will point the way to a (desired) conclusion? The source of the consensus is unidentified, but obviously it refers to Canadian and American academic critics of the U.S.
system, whose habit it is to cite each other as sources. Another aspect
of the alleged consensus is the role of unions as well as employers:
"Canadian employers and unions are both more willing to accept one
another and commit themselves more directly and blindingly
[bindingly?] to political parties" (Huxley, Kettler, and Struthers 1986,
116). Perhaps there is a softer glove over the steel hand in Canada, but
style is not substance.

An investigation of managerial acceptance of unions and bargaining
in Canada, based on surveys of "senior executives" and secondary
sources, found "little interest in displacing existing unions" and relatively fewer unfair labor practices charges against employers in Canada
than in the United States (Verma and Thompson 1989, 259). As for "senior executives" reporting "little interest in displacing unions," can one
imagine any other response? Aside from the risk of committing an unfair labor practice under various Canadian laws by a contrary admission

(the confidentiality of surveys notwithstanding), any senior executives who would declare the company's policies in favor of ousting unions would themselves very likely be ousted. Aside from legal hazards, it would be poor form in the company culture.

As for the relatively greater number of unfair labor practices in the United States than in Canada, like the aggregate figures on unionism, these data are at best overstatements, at worst misleading. In scrutinizing some of Weiler's conclusions based on this data, LaLonde and Meltzer claim that the data overstate or mislead because the relevant section of U.S. law on which they are based "extends far beyond the organizational context . . . [and] during the 1960s, interpretations . . . generated new grounds for back pay orders for large numbers of employees, as a remedy for misconduct in contexts far removed from organizational campaigns." As a result, "[t]hose developments raise a serious question about Professor Weiler's estimate of the percentage of back pay and reinstatement orders that arose from employer misconduct (actual or alleged) calculated to block a union's securing majority support" (LaLonde and Meltzer 1991, 967). Finally, in order to compare the two countries on unfair labor practices, those practices that are actually the product of illegal conduct affecting organization must be reviewed in terms of administrative regulations as well as employment. Counts alone are not an adequate basis for a comparative analysis.

In sharp contrast to the alleged attitude of "senior executives," when Canadian union leaders were interviewed about Canadian management's acceptance of unions and bargaining, their responses were completely at odds with the consensus mythology. (No confidentiality was required since the labor leaders would not be charged with unfair labor practices and were apparently eager to let their views be known.) The consensus of twelve major Canadian union leaders, interviewed (in about 1986–87) by two pro-union industrial relations specialists on a variety of issues affecting Canadian unionism in the 1980s, was that management, including, unsurprisingly, some in the public sector, vigorously opposed unions. Indeed, as the editors' summary of the interview stated: "Most labour leaders don't think employers accept the legitimacy of unions [and] [t]here has been no change in employer attitudes toward unions or in supervisor attitudes toward workers" (Kumar and Ryan 1988, 9). Obviously, then, employer opposition was not only current in the 1980s, but was long standing. In examining Canadian unions' inability to organize banking, a major nonunion stronghold in the private sector, Kumar and Ryan commented that "the most important [obstacle was] the employers' fierce anti-union attitude, their determination to stay nonunion at any cost" (1988, 12). Because of their suspicions of employer attitudes and policies, the surveyed union leaders opposed employee participatory programs such as quality of work life, quality circles, team concepts, or employee involvement and flexibility in work arrangements, viewing them as "nothing but a misguided desire for a union free environment" (Kumar and Ryan 1988, 8). Shades of the American industrial relations system! Perhaps most important, these findings signify that the mainstreamers have overlooked the attitudes of supervisors, the managers who deal with union representatives daily and intimately, in contrast to "senior executives," who in public or in a confidential survey may wax "philosophical."

Not only do many Canadian employers oppose unionization (after all, many of them are headquartered in the United States and why should they behave differently north of the border?), but the public at large is actually more hostile to organized labor in Canada than in the United States. As astounding as it may seem, in view of the conventional wisdom about American anti-unionism, "more Canadians than Americans view unions as too powerful; more Canadians than Americans perceive labor as the greatest threat; fewer Canadians than Americans have confidence in labor as an institution; more Canadians than Americans blame unions for inflation and Americans are more likely to express approval of unions than Canadians" (Lipset 1990, 8). Such findings undermine claims of divergence of results in Canadian and American labor relations.

Concession Bargaining

Another putative divergence in the divergent model, one related to employer opposition, was the so-called tougher position taken by Canadian than American unions on concession bargaining in the 1980s (Perusek 1989). Putting aside the fact that Canadian unions and industry were sheltered behind a higher tariff barrier than their American counterparts in that time period, were Canadian unions tougher in the 1980s? According to Kumar and Ryan and the union leadership they interviewed: "[a]lthough they have accepted lower wage settlements, even wage cuts, wage freezes and elimination of COLA [cost of living adjustment] clauses where employers have been hard hit by recession and experiencing weak and uncertain economic recovery, unions have taken a strong position on 'concession bargaining' and have refused to give in on management demands for permanent changes in wage structures and work rules without appropriate job and union security guarantees" (Kumar and Ryan 1988, 8). If there is a distinction between the United States and Canada in concession bargaining during the 1980s, it is a distinction without a difference. The claim of Canadian unionists and many academics that U.S. unions "gave in" is invidious, nationalistic rhetoric. Thus, the research director of the International Union, United Automobile Workers, AFL-CIO, characterized remarks that the UAW leadership in the United States "worked hand-in-hand with corporations to provide concessions" in the 1980s as "slanderous and at variance with the facts" (Friedman 1989, 4). Of all American unions, it is not hyperbole to say that the UAW has always stood in the forefront of union militancy.

Empirically, the facts contradict the characterization of American unions' flabbiness compared to the Canadians during the 1980s. Statistically, Canadian unions' ability to raise wages relative to nonunion workers ranked below that of the American unions, 1985–87, according to Blanchflower and Freeman (1990). As their report showed, a reputedly weaker union movement actually raised members' compensation more than the allegedly more robust one!

Another strand in the comparative bargaining issue is implied by Kochan's thesis of "strategic choice," that is, union participation in management decisions affecting investment, or what I would simply term his version of co-determination. Kochan and Verma agree that the two countries' systems are different, and that their "institutional responses . . . appear to be somewhat different, with the Canadian being more stable." I interpret this to mean either that union membership and density have held up better in Canada than in the United States, in which case this is but another repetition of the false comparison of union membership and density, or that the Canadian system has been in some other way more durable. However, continue Kochan and Verma, this stability will be undermined if incremental adjustment to innovation by management and unions proves too slow, or "if Canadian union leaders choose not to champion a broader role in decision making within firms." If they do not, say Kochan and Verma, "we expect Canadian managers to become more disillusioned with unions and collective bargaining and to accelerate their search for nonunion options" (Kochan and Verma 1989, 81, 91). Aside from being a non sequitur conclusion dependent on an improbable premise, the evidence of union leaders desiring to engage in "strategic decision making" is no more than a rhetorical call for works councils, a position Kochan has and continues to champion. Its likelihood is no greater north of the 49th parallel than south of it. Thus, Kumar and Ryan reported no Canadian union leaders suggesting or desiring anything remotely associated with the "strategic choice" option. Quite the contrary, they found that "[l]abour leaders strongly believe in the adversarial system of labour relations citing the fundamentally different roles of union and management at the workplace" (Kumar and Ryan 1988, 9). As for management, since so many key firms in Canada are subsidiaries of U.S.-owned companies, companies that resolutely oppose union participation in "strategic decision making" in the United States, is it likely that they, or Canadian companies, will see matters any differently north of the border? Equally important, U.S. union leadership shares the adversarial view of Canadian union leaders and rejects "strategic decision making" as a strategy for recovering membership.

The Canadian Public Sector Industrial Relations System

The fingerprints of labor law on public sector industrial relations are ubiquitous in both countries, but far more heavily in Canada than in the United States. This complements the larger Canadian public labor market and is the sufficient condition for stimulating the New Unionism. It is also another major divergence in the (public sector) industrial relations systems of the two countries and again producing convergent trends. To understand the special role of law in the Canadian system, consider the elements of an organized industrial relations system—management (in this case the government), government (as lawmaker), public employees, and unions. In Canada, federal and provincial governments have so merged their functions as the sovereign and the employers to ensure collective bargaining on an scale exceeding any G-7 country. As lawmaker and employer, Canadian governments have often *statutorily* decided the scope of the bargaining unit, the bargaining partner, and in many instances key terms of the agreement itself, notably compulsory membership and dues collection. Mainstream critics of American private policy (justifiably) complain when employers illegally interfere with employees' freedom of choice, but are silent or justify Canadian policy mandating employees' representatives.

In none of the governmental jurisdictions in the United States—the federal government, the states, and their subdivisions—is there a comparable policy. The American system is therefore much more open to competing labor organizations and to workers' freedom of choice, including the choice of no union representation. To date, I am unfamiliar with any advocacy to apply Canadian public sector policy to the United States. The reason, I am sure, is that the Canadian public system—selecting representatives and providing for compulsory membership and dues payments, and denying employee choice—would receive little or no legislative support.

While Canadian public policy is also more interventionist in the public than in the private labor market, paradoxically, the less interventionist private policy reinforces the demand for more interventionist policy in the government labor market. Because private sector law applies to many public sector workers in Canada, it justifies the demand of all other public unions for equality of treatment—"full collective bargaining rights" —in their dealings with the government employer. Application of private law to public employees has contributed significantly to full collective bargaining in the public sector in several ways. Not the least of these is to proclaim that there is no difference in the relationship between employers and employees in the two sectors. For example, if the right to strike is permissible for employees (public and private) who are subject to private policy, it legitimizes the claim to the same right of public employees under public law. Likewise, the same standard can reasonably be claimed for the scope of bargaining, compulsory membership, and the check-off.

Before proceeding further, however, three prerequisites are required for understanding the application of Canadian policy to the public—and for that matter, the private—labor markets. The first is the division of the constitutional jurisdiction between federal and provincial labor law. Thus, there are eleven jurisdictions (ignoring municipal governments, although these are important, too) enacting law for the public and private sectors. Between the federal and provincial jurisdictions, the provincial law accounts for most, perhaps 90 percent, of total employment (Meltz 1990, 48). Moreover, provincial law has typically been more sweeping in favoring unionism, even though federal law has often set precedents. (Similar relationships exist in the United States; the local and state governments employ more workers than the federal government, and their policies, overall, are more pro-union than are the federal.)

Second, the application of policy to the public sector varies substantially within each of the jurisdictions. At the federal level, most employees are covered by a single public sector law, and the balance by federal private sector law. At the provincial level, public employees performing different functions may be subject to several public sector laws or a single private law.

Third, many public employees in Canada are subject to private law. Thus, employees of crown corporations are subject to private law, while those of crown agencies are under the jurisdiction of public law. Privatized enterprises previously subject to private law continue under private law. Air Canada is an example. In the United States, the only public employees subject to private law are employees of the U.S. Postal Service. They were transferred to the jurisdiction of private law, the National Labor Relations Act, in 1970. By that time, postal workers, comprising the largest single unit of employment in the economy, were also one of the most unionized groups in the entire labor market, some 70 percent in 2002, so there is little application of the Act to postal employees' organizational efforts. Under the NLRA the postal unions have nearly the same bargaining rights as private employees. Pensions remain outside the scope of bargaining, but given the richness of the benefits, this is hardly a limitation. Postal employees are also forbidden to strike and subject to arbitration.

Another group subject to private law in the United States is employees of what I term quasi-public enterprises. By quasi-public I mean, for example, nonprofit hospitals that derive much, perhaps most, of their revenue from public funds. On the other hand, employees of the Tennessee Valley Authority, a federal agency and therefore subject to federal policy, long ago adopted and applied the procedures of private policy (the NLRA), but are not subject to it. This may also be true of the government shipyards. Roughly, these groups are analogous to crown corporations in Canada in being subject to private law. All told, in the United States the crossover of private policy to public enterprises and employees is minuscule in a civilian labor force exceeding 122 million. Clearly, Canadian and American policies diverge in their applications to public employment.

Although all Canadian provinces share intrusive policies, within them there is considerable variation in jurisdictional application (Ponak and Thompson 1989, 386–91). At one end is Ontario, with several policies for public employees. General municipal employees and hospital workers are covered by the same provincial law as private sector employees, although hospital employees are also subject to special legislation dealing with the arbitration of disputes. All other employees of the province are subject to separate legislation applicable to their function.

In contrast to Ontario, most of Quebec's public employees are covered by the same law as private sector employees, the Quebec Labour Code. In addition, special provisions for public employees supplement the Code. The other eight provinces fall somewhere in between Ontario and Quebec. Within those eight, there is considerable variation, as for example on policies toward provincial crown employees. About half of these provinces have enacted special legislation for crown corporations and half have placed them under private sector law.

The influence of private sector labor law on rights of "full collective bargaining" for public employees shows up in collective bargaining agreements providing for compulsory union membership. These have had a dramatic effect on membership, especially among municipal workers (Rose 1984, 104–5). Further amplification of public sector unions' power is seen in some educational jurisdictions, which not only statutorily identify the bargaining agent, but also compel membership as a condition of employment. Five provinces, including Ontario, statutorily compel membership among teachers, with some exceptions, and they have the right to strike. Membership is made compulsory "with some exceptions, and is now a condition of employment for virtually all teachers working in Ontario" (Simmons and Swan 1982, 61). These extraordinary practices were justified because of the "need to effect the transition to collective bargaining quickly, avoiding certification proceedings while the [collective bargaining] regime [was] being implemented" in the public sector (Simmons and Swan 1982, 64). Not surprisingly, in just two years, 1971–73, Canadian union membership in education jumped 560 percent, and then added another 50 percent over the next five years (Rose 1984, 107). In other jurisdictions, compulsory membership is negotiated in closed shop (membership is a condition of hire as well as tenure of employment) or union shop (a condition of tenure of employment) agreements. The agency shop, in which there is payment of the equivalent of dues without the requirement of membership, accommodates those individuals who object to union membership for religious or philosophical reasons.

Policy applicable to crown agencies followed the pattern of general government in establishing bargaining units and agents. For example, Ontario's Crown Employees Collective Bargaining Act of 1972 identified the bargaining unit and agent for crown agencies established before the Act. For crown agencies established after the enactment of the 1972 law, the Ontario Public Service Labour Relations Tribunal establishes the unit and certifies the bargaining agent upon application by unions. And application does not necessarily require a representation election; a check of membership cards, representing 55 percent of the employees in the proposed unit, suffices. Similar grants of recognition have occurred in some state jurisdictions in the United States. However, such practices were altered in the U.S. private sector under the amended National Labor Relations Act of 1947. American experience had shown that coercion and peer pressure at mass meetings were often instrumental in obtaining applications for membership subsequently presented to the National Labor Relations Board as evidence of employee wishes for representation. Currently, unions and their academic supporters seek the reintroduction of the procedure wholesale as a way of reviving union membership. The divergences between the two countries' industrial relations systems on determining and certifying bargaining units and representatives, as well as some key terms of the agreement, explain much of the markedly higher public density rates in Canada.

Historically, U.S. policies at the federal level initiated the expansion of public unionism in the United States and Canada as well. President Kennedy's Executive order 10988 of 1962 preceded the Quebec (1964) and the Canadian federal government's (1967) enactments. Because of Kennedy's order, and its emulation by many state and local governments (actually, New York City and the State of Wisconsin adopted policies that preceded the Order), the New Unionism grew rapidly. In Canada, Saskatchewan gave public employees the right to organize and strike in 1944, but its policies had little significance for the contemporary public union movement. The Canadian version of the New Unionism really got under way in the 1960s, emulating the American experience, and followed the enactments of Quebec and the federal government.

The process of growth of the New Unionism was also common to both countries, a process I call "organizing the organized." Organizing the unorganized, the typical method of unionization, has been the exception, not the rule, in the public labor markets of both countries. Existing public employee and professional associations converted themselves into collective bargaining organizations and accounted for the major part, if not the majority, of the new public union movement. Indeed, the largest public sector union in the United States, and in fact the largest union, private or public in North America, is a former professional association, the National Education Association.

The association-to-union transformation in the United States was emulated in Canada at both the federal and provincial levels (Rose 1984, 99). Statutory recognition of the associations as the bargaining representative, especially of teachers, was a major factor hastening the conversion of Canada's associations into unions. In effect, the association-to-union transformation in such instances was automatic or as, Canadians describe it, "instant unionism."

As the new, giant public sector union movement unfolded in Canada, the public sector industrial relations system quickly took on those characteristics of the private system ("full collective bargaining") to a degree far exceeding practices in this country. In particular I refer to compulsory membership, the right to strike, and the power to negotiate the terms and conditions of employment—wages, working conditions, holidays, vacations, and health and safety conditions. Not on the bargaining table in Canada are managerial rights (as in the private sector) and civil service procedures such as recruitment and job classification. Even so, "non-negotiable" items have been the subject of "letters of understanding" (Goldenberg 1988, 294). In many governmental jurisdictions, promotion, demotion, transfer, layoff, and recall are negotiable. What remains of the civil service systems in both countries is moot.

Another aspect of "full collective bargaining rights" is the right of public sector unions to strike in many jurisdictions in Canada. By contrast, legal sanction to strike is more the exception than the rule in the United States. The right to strike in Canada varies across and within the eleven public sector jurisdictions (Ponak and Thompson 1989, 387). For example, Manitoba permits municipal employees, police, and hospital workers to strike, while teachers, firefighters, and civil servants must submit to arbitration. In Quebec, on the other hand, police and firefighters cannot strike and must submit to arbitration, while all other functions may strike. This has hardly inhibited strikes by public sector employees in Quebec, the province experiencing the worst strike record, measured in time lost, between 1973 and 1985 (Ponak and Thompson 1989, 393). In Ontario, local government employees are covered by private law and have the right to strike, while provincial employees who are subject to public sector law do not. Teachers have the right to strike, but employees in health care do not.

Canadian policy toward public unions was not made just by statutory enactments. In crown corporations, managerial policy added significantly to the strength and power of Canada's New Unionism. While public enterprises "are commercial entities with objectives similar to private firms . . . in addition, they are policy instruments with a requirement to pursue government objectives" (Economic Council of Canada 1986, 2). The Council described government ownership of enterprises in Canada as an expression of a "concept of the positive interventionist state." Notwithstanding that the managements of crown corporations may conduct their enterprises as do private employers, can there be any doubt that one objective of the interventionist state is the encouragement of collective bargaining?

Market forces—privatization and subcontracting—potentially pose a serious challenge to the New Unionism in Canada (in the United States, as well). However, the continued expansion in the density of the New Unionism indicates it is more potential than real. In some sectors publicly owned enterprises dominate or occupy a major position in the industry. Measured by employment, public production of electric power in Canada may yet account for over 80 percent of the industry's employment; likewise, perhaps over 40 percent of employment in communications and nearly that percentage in transportation employment. In 1985, there were over 500 government-owned or -controlled enterprises, over 80 by the federal government, and the remainder accounted for by provincial and local governments (Economic Council of Canada 1986). Publicly owned establishments in Canada encompass such giant enterprises as Ontario Hydro, the largest nonfinancial company in Canada (by size of assets); Quebec Hydro; and numerous others in telephones, utilities, and mining; and, until it was privatized, Air Canada. In theory, privatization in Canada could bring the Canadian economic structure closer to the American, but, in practice, privatization's effects on unionism occur slowly.

Policies for privatization are extant at the federal level and in some of the provinces. While ministries for privatization apparently do not exist at the provincial level, the Liberal Party in Ontario adopted a position favoring some privatization, and the Province of Saskatchewan has cooperated with the federal government to merge and privatize into one company their respective holdings in two uranium mining companies. Most of the privatization to date has been at the federal level, leaving the bulk of public enterprises, which are at the provincial and municipal level, untouched. Within three years of the election of the Conservative government in 1984, the federal government privatized eleven companies including Canadair, deHaviland, and Teleglobe Canada. Privatization in transportation has been stimulated by increased deregulation, a policy given impetus by the U.S. deregulation of airlines that began in 1978.

As yet, privatization has had little impact on density in the public sector in Canada. When privatization occurs, if the applicable labor relations policy was already private, the policy remains unchanged. Presumably, if government sector policy applied, the privatized company becomes subject to private law. If so, initially, privatization increases private density, as I have pointed out above, because private management requires time to reshape its work force. Whether or not privatization will eventually lead to lower union penetration of a company depends mainly on the restructuring of employment. I expect that as technological and market forces reshape the occupational composition of employment, more professional, technical, and managerial employees will be added and most of these are likely to be nonunion, as is characteristic of the private labor market. In general, therefore, there should be a slow and small downward drift in the unionization rate of privatized companies. However, the scale effect is bound to be small. In the long run, privatization will be reinforced by the Free Trade Agreement (FTA) between the United States and Canada, but its impact will likely be apparent only after a considerable interval. The FTA's main effects eventually will be felt among organized private enterprises—that is, by lowering private density.

Increased public ownership of Canadian industry during the 1960s and 1970s put the New Unionism in Canada on a track of expansion that continues to a point approaching saturation in the new century: Public ownership "became an increasingly popular form of [state] intervention" in Canada (Economic Council of Canada 1986, 20). Even more decisive for the New Unionism was the growth of employment education, health, and welfare services. The confluence of these trends led the mainstream to find a historic crossover in the trend of *average density* between Canada and the United States (Weiler 1983, 1818; Huxley, Kettler, and Struthers 1986, 119, for example). The alleged crossover became a celebrated turning point in the divergent-divergent argument. Ever since this "finding," the mainstream has claimed that Canadian and American trends "have been progressing along quite different trajectories" (Huxley, Kettler, and Struthers 1986, 117). It also gave birth to the myth that the United States was unique among major nations in the decline of private unionism. In reality, as Canadian private density ebbed, the surge of Canadian public unionism generated the celebrated crossover, as my analysis has shown. Instead of "progressing along different trajectories," Canadian and American trends in private density have been progressing along similar trends, as postulated by my convergence model, albeit with the Canadian lagging.

Once dominated by blue collar private sector unions, now mainly white collar public sector unions dominate the Canadian union movement. In the short span of ten years the relative strength of the two union groups was reversed. Based on my calculations of private and public sector membership and densities, in 1975 the private sector membership accounted for 58 percent of the total; in a complete turnaround, by 1985 public sector unions accounted for 56 percent of total membership (Troy 1990). Based on Statistics Canada's Labour Force Surveys (which I believe overstate private unionism), in 2002 the New Unionism in Canada accounts for 52.5 percent of total membership, while accounting for only 22.3 percent of employment; in other words, even by the official data, Canadian New Unionism is nearly two and one-half times its proportion in employment. As I have already noted, the Canadian public union movement is doubtless the largest (in relative terms) of all G-7 countries.

The Canadian Private Sector Industrial Relations System

Canadian and American policies differ markedly in their degree of intervention in labor markets, private as well as public. In Canada, policy is much more interventionist in its public than in its private sector, but policies in the private sector do not lag far behind. Although the law does not identify the bargaining representative as in the public sector, in all but three jurisdictions (Nova Scotia, Alberta, and British Columbia), Canadian labor boards can certify a union as the bargaining representative and require employers to recognize and negotiate based on a card check; that is, evidence that a majority of the employees in the prospective bargaining unit have signed up as members of the union (Carter 1988, 34). In Ontario a showing of 55 percent of the prospective bargaining unit suffices to warrant recognition. In other provinces and the federal jurisdiction, the showing of interest need only be a simple majority. That such narrow margins, despite labor board rules to ensure authenticity, suffice to award recognition demonstrates the intent of public authorities to assist the growth of unions in Canada. One cannot conceive of an analogous procedure in civic elections, from which the American and Canadian industrial relations system borrowed the principle of majority determination. It is all the more egregious since the card check procedure is, in fact, the usual method of gaining representation in Canada. Indeed, the secret ballot choice of a representative is "a secondary procedure . . . used by labour boards only if there is some doubt about the reliability of the membership evidence submitted by the union" (Carter 1989, 34–35). In the United States, the secret ballot election is the standard and preferred practice. The benefit to union ranks of the Canadian procedure is significant because it avoids the true test of workers' support of the union—the secret ballot. When elections are held, they are conducted soon after application for certification and are not subject to delays, which are frequently long in the United States. This is held to be a virtue of the Canadian system and a deficiency of the American one. Doubtless the speed of the Canadian system helps unions win recognition, but does that also ensure confidence in the workers' true wishes? For despite quickie elections and related procedures benefiting organization and bargaining, currently no more than 18 percent of private sector Canadian workers actually belong to unions. This indicates that policy in Canada, as well as in the United States, is based on the questionable assumption that nonunion workers want unions and only employers stand in their way. This has, indeed, been the gospel in the United States despite repeated polls of nonunion workers that demonstrate a lack of interest in union representation (Farber 1989; Troy 1990). Indeed, the sliding proportion of organized private workers in both countries also raises a question about the real desire of public workers for unions: Is their high level of participation more a function of policy than a desire to join unions?

Another important objection to the card check procedure is that it can influence, even determine, the scope of the bargaining unit, a significant factor affecting the outcome of an election to unionize an enterprise. In defining the bargaining unit, a labor board (Canadian or U.S.) can rely on the extent of organization (membership cards) as the standard and thereby predetermine the outcome of an election. In U.S. civic elections this is termed "gerrymandering." Meanwhile, it should be noted that workers' support for unions has decreased in Britain, too (Phelps Brown 1990).

When illegal managerial opposition to organization is present in the United States, the National Labor Relations Board first purges that illegal influence and then conducts an election. In Canada, boards can certify the union in such instances. Also, in contrast to U.S. law, Canadian labor boards can levy punitive fines; in contrast, U.S. workers are made "whole" in earnings and employment as a result of illegal employer interference.

Canadian labor boards limit employers' communications with employees much more closely than their U.S. counterparts. Like the card checks, the practice emulates the earlier procedures of the U.S. National Labor Relations Board:

> A particular concern of labour boards is statements made by employers while unions are organizing. Close attention is paid not only to the content of such statements but also to the context in which they are made. (Carter 1989, 38)

Under the original version of the National Labor Relations Act and its administration, employers complained that their rights of free speech under the Bill of Rights of the U.S. Constitution were abridged by activist labor boards then practicing what is apparently now standard in Canada. When the Act was amended in 1947, protection of employer communication with employees was added so long as it did not include threats of reprisals or promises of reward. In Canada, some jurisdictions have gone well beyond the original American practice and legislated the requirement that employers *disprove* anti-union attitudes. One can only ask, what happened to the Anglo-Saxon common law doctrine of the presumption of innocence until proven guilty? And how does one prove a negative? Furthermore, employer violations are even subject to criminal prosecution, although the practice is said to be rare.

Labor boards in the federal jurisdiction and in Manitoba, Newfoundland, and Ontario also have the power to determine the first agreement in bargaining disputes after a union is certified as the employees' representative; these agreements are binding for one year. In Quebec, when a "significant percentage" of workers favors union representation, the province's procedures certify the union and then allow the union to apply for a decree that requires the application of the same terms and conditions of employment subsequently negotiated to nonunion workers in the same occupation or region. No parallels for these procedures are to be found in any jurisdiction in the United States, or apparently elsewhere in Canada.

Canadian labor law also permits private sector unions to negotiate closed, union, and agency shop provisions in collective bargaining agreements.

Only individuals voicing religious objections can opt out of membership. Nominally, closed shops are illegal in the United States, but in reality not in the industries in which they were historically important, such as construction and the longshore and maritime trades. The union and agency shops are legal across the United States, except in right-to-work states, which ban such agreements. Railways and airlines, which are governed by the Railway Labor Act, are not subject to state right-to-work legislation and therefore in these industries the parties may negotiate agreements requiring compulsory membership as a condition of employment in all states. Needless to say, there are no Canadian equivalents of U.S. state laws banning compulsory membership. Indeed, just the opposite applies in some Canadian jurisdictions, where laws mandate the agency shop and employers' collection of union dues and fees, even from nonmembers. Other jurisdictions do require that employees first authorize the dues deduction, as in the United States.

Like the requirements for compulsory membership or agency shop, unions in the private system of industrial relations are strengthened by legal requirements to establish grievance machinery to settle disputes over the terms of an existing agreement. It is not a matter for the parties to negotiate, as in the United States, although, in fact, the practice is universal in America. More important, in Canada the arbitration award is not ordinarily subject to judicial review. Only in the event an arbitrator exceeded his jurisdiction or reached a decision that was "patently unreasonable" can a court intervene; practice in the United States is similar.

In addition to grievance arbitration, Canadian law provides for arbitration of new terms of employment in an impasse (interest arbitration). Even though the procedure may not be widely used, it is yet another example of the intrusive nature of Canadian policy in the private sector; this is absent in the United States, except in some jurisdictions in the public system.

At the federal level, private employers and crown corporations (subject to private law) that are preparing to introduce technological changes "likely to affect the terms and conditions of employment of a significant number of employees, shall give [written] notice of the proposed changes to the bargaining agent at least 120 days beforehand" (Commerce Clearing House 1989, 393). These must detail the anticipated impact of the intended changes. The union then petitions the Canadian Labour Relations Board for authority to negotiate the anticipated effects of the change. Until that is satisfied, no technological change may be introduced, unless the Board decides that the employer need not negotiate the change. Technological changes require, therefore, a significant measure of bureaucratic input, hardly an encouragement to innovation. Essentially, technological changes are left to collective bargaining in the United States.

The Free Trade Agreement

The Canadian-U.S. FTA went into effect on January 1, 1989; elimination of all tariffs between the two countries is to be phased in over ten years. The agreement includes services as well as goods and liberalizes cross-national investment flows. In facilitating business travel between the two countries, it will also encourage the movement of labor and therefore of human capital (Royal Bank of Canada 1990, 3). The FTA has since been followed by the North American Free Trade Agreement between Mexico, Canada, and the United States, which will increase market pressures on unions in all three countries.

The Free Trade Agreement (FTA) can be expected to increase convergence between Canada and the United States not only in industrial relations outcomes, but perhaps even in the systems themselves. Of course, Canadian private sector industrial relations have always been subject to competitive forces, but in the past the Canadian system was shielded from imports to a greater extent than the American. Within Canada, provincial law has also protected intraprovincial union groups by procurement policies favoring local suppliers and local content. Prior to the FTA, Canadian tariffs substantially exceeded U.S. tariffs. On average, Canadian tariff rates on U.S. goods, weighted by value of the traded products, were more than five times American tariff rates on Canadian imports, 3.8 percent to 0.7 percent (Little 1988, Table 3, 8). The Royal Bank of Canada reported that on the eve of the FTA, "the average Canadian tariff of dutiable goods stood . . . at 6.5 percent on U.S. goods" (Royal Bank of Canada 1991, 6). Even Canadian unions in new car and car parts manufacturing were in a favored position relative to the United States, because of the duty-free auto pact of 1965. As a result of that agreement, which committed the U.S. manufacturers to minimum levels of production in Canada, the previous comparative disadvantage of Canadian auto production was reduced if not converted to an advantage through lower labor costs, enhanced by economies of scale, and a sharply depreciated Canadian dollar relative to the U.S. dollar,

1978–1984. Canadian employment and unionism in the industry prospered, while in the United States auto employment and membership fell. Significantly, except for one local union, the Canadian wing of the Auto Workers union seceded from the International in 1983 when, after benefiting from sheltered market forces, its leadership asserted it would not agree to the concessions the U.S.-based international, at a competitive disadvantage with the Canadian auto industry, had accepted. More than any other transnational event, this is the one that gave rise to the invidious charge by academics that U.S. unions were not as "tough" as their Canadian counterparts.

The effects of the FTA on unions on both sides of the border are bound to be substantial given the enormous volume of trade between the two countries. The United States accounts for 75 percent of Canadian exports, or one-quarter of Canada's gross national product (Crispo 1990), and most American direct investment overseas goes to Canada (Little 1988, 6–7). Because of the very extensive U.S. role in the Canadian economy, and for political reasons, the initiative for the FTA had to come from Canada, not the United States, otherwise it "would have been the kiss of death; free trade would have been interpreted in Canada as a U.S. scheme to extend its economic hegemony" (Wonnacott 1990, 4).

6

IS THE DEMOCRATIC PARTY
THE LABOR PARTY
OF THE UNITED STATES?

> It's like night and day comparing the AFL-CIO's political
> operations today with those in the 1994 elections. It's like
> comparing a Model T with a Ferrari.
> —*Charles Cook, political analyst*[1]

Origin of the Argument

My answer to the question posed by this chapter's title is yes. Labor
parties have appeared periodically throughout American history, but they
have always been minor and transitory; such will not be the case with
the newly born Labor Party of the United States because it wears the
clothes of the oldest political party of the country—the Democratic Party.
I am not the first to equate the Labor Movement with the Democratic
Party, but I did so independently. Several years ago, columnist William
Safire wrote: "The Democratic Party is now America's Labor Party,"
because the AFL-CIO rounded up enough Democratic congressmen to
deny President Clinton fast-track authority to negotiate foreign trade
agreements without congressional authority (Safire 1997). Safire explained that "John Sweeney, boss of the AFL-CIO, made it happen. He
proved he had the money, the troops and the clout within the Democratic Party to call the shots" (1997). He then wrote that Clinton acknowledged the unions' power when the president observed, "I wish we
could have had a secret vote [on fast-track authorization] in the Congress—we'd pass it 3 or 4 to 1." His comment was interpreted by many
House Democrats to mean that they sold their votes for union money or
feared union punishment; it was not cordially received by them.

I have added significant facts and analysis to Safire's characterization of the Democratic Party as the Labor Party of the United States. In
particular, I have pointed to the union leadership's practice of using not
only the compelled dues and fees of all members and nonmembers they
represent to support candidates and policies they favored, but their even
larger in-kind contributions to the Democrats. The monies from members' and workers' dues and fees are described as "compelled" because
they are collected under union or agency shop agreements requiring
payment as a condition of employment. Despite the fact that *all* workers
covered by such agreements fund the Democratic Party, *37 percent voted
for Bush and against policies their leaders favored.* Meanwhile, the AFL-
CIO claims that surveys of members support their choice of candidates'
policies. Yet, the Federation has never publicly disclosed the methods,
reliability of sample, and results of these surveys.

From Trade Union to Political Partner

Because the Old Unionism is in decline and seeks political solutions to
its trade union problems, and the New Unionism automatically merges
its trade union with its political function, the American Labor Movement has shifted it focus and resources increasingly to the political function. Quantitatively, this has been established by the Supreme Court's
decision in *Communications Workers v. Beck*, 487 U.S. 735 (1988), a
private sector case, which determined that the union spent 79 percent of
its revenue on matters unrelated to unions' trade union functions. In the
public sector, a lower court in *Lehnert v. Ferris Faculty Association*, 643
F. Sup 1306 (1986), found that the Michigan Education Association and
its parent, the National Education Association, spent 3.4 and 2.75 percent of their revenues, respectively, for bargaining and contract administration, the balance going to other purposes. (The local union, in
contrast, spent 81 percent on these matters, as might be expected of a
local organization.) Those other purposes include political activity. Both
wings of the Labor Movement allocate great amounts of money, organizational structure, and personnel to their political activities; the propor-
tions are greater in the New Unionism. The Old Unionism may be in
decline in membership and density, but it is still the largest in the world,
and its income and wealth are also the largest worldwide, exceeding
those of the New Unionism. The New Unionism stands at record levels
in membership and density, making it, too, the largest in membership,

income, and wealth among government employees worldwide. Combined, the Old and the New Unionism enroll some 16 million members, number probably 45,000 separate organizations, command an income of $13–14 billion, and have assets in excess of $10 billion. Because of that population, organizational strength, wealth, and income, the American Labor Movement's connections to the Democratic Party make it the power center of the Party.

The Labor Movement's strength goes beyond its known financial resources. In fact, it is the magnitude of the Labor Movement's in-kind contributions to the Democrats that sets it apart from any other contributors and groups within the Party. By in-kind contributions, I mean the unions' pro-Democratic press going to 16 million members each month, uniformly supporting the Party's candidates and positions, paid for by members' compelled dues and fees (in fact, the union media is so biased in favor of the Democratic Party that it is no exaggeration to characterize it as a one-party press); the use of cyberspace and other methods to enroll voters and get out the vote; electioneering by thousands of union members and employees of unions, whether or not they receive their regular pay; provision of data and telephone banks on voters; voter tracking and polling; transporting voters to the polls; subsidizing delegates and alternates to political conventions; exchanging research and strategy decisions with the Democratic Party; direct mail to members in comparing candidates' voting profiles, which almost universally caricature Republican candidates; providing platforms for public personalities sympathetic to the Democratic Party, at no cost to the Party; and pack rallies with members and employees for Democratic candidates. At times, unions close or reduce operations for a period of time prior to an election in order to send their staff out to work for Democrats, again, at no cost to the Party and, again, without consultation of the members whom that staff are paid to serve. The unions also sell (!) election campaign buttons to members, buttons that urge votes for Democratic Party candidates.

An example of the extent of unions' in-kind contributions was Election Day, November 7, 2000. Election Day was a paid holiday in Michigan for the Auto Workers under agreements reached with the employers. This enabled thousands of unionists to work on behalf of the Democratic Party at no cost to the Party. An example of the unions' use of cyberspace to get out the vote in Michigan was the operation of a high-tech phone bank outside the headquarters of the state AFL-CIO. It was operated by volunteers who were members of a local of the Service Employees International Union, Sweeney's former union and one of the most activist in the union movement. They used a computer-driven dialing system to contact union members and retirees, whose names then appeared on a screen. If a person answered, the volunteer came on line to make the case for the Democratic ticket. If it was an answering machine, the volunteer clicked a mouse to leave a taped message from the president of the state AFL-CIO. Every member of an AFL-CIO affiliated union was scheduled to receive at least two pieces of mail and at least two phone calls (Edsall 2000). These activities did not include the electioneering of the National Education Association, the largest union in the country, because it is not affiliated with the AFL-CIO; but it too was active in Michigan and across the country.

Nationally, the AFL-CIO political director estimated that in the 2000 election 1,000 union officials worked full time on the election, while individual unions supplied more than 100,000 volunteers for phone banks, weekend door knocking, and Election Day canvassing. His estimate of the number of volunteers should be treated as the minimum: nationally, the Democrats benefited from the services of the staff of many of the larger subordinate unions across the country, augmented by untold numbers of members and retirees. In general, the ability of unions to implement their in-kind contributions to the Democratic Party is enhanced by the structure of the union movement. Contrary to popular and media notions, the union movement is not the AFL-CIO on 16th Street in Washington, D.C.; the Federation is the proverbial tip of the iceberg. The union movement consists of about 45,000 subordinate unions, including some 2,000 or so intermediate bodies distributed across the country, and perhaps 100 regional, national, and international headquarter bodies. Unions' total income is nearly evenly divided among the 45,000 subordinate unions and their parent bodies. Locals control about 47 percent of unions' total revenue and assets, while the parent unions' shares account for 40 percent of revenue and 42 percent of assets; intermediate organizations account for the balance (all financial figures are for 1995; Masters and Atkin 1997, Table 1, 494). Hence, it is clear that unions' power to generate in-kind contributions is widely spread across the country and therefore in a position to benefit the Democratic Party *at all political levels*. Together with all other in-kind contributions, I have estimated the value of these resources in a presidential election cycle at $300 million; to this must be added the cash contributions, which in

1996 amounted to $100 million, bringing the total value of the unions' contributions to the Democratic Party in 1996 to $400 million (Troy 2000). A similar, if not larger, amount was undoubtedly expended in the 2000 election and should be expected in 2004.

The Value of Unions' In-Kind Contributions

The purpose of unions' spending, cash and in-kind, is to acquire the services of the Democratic Party for policy and other legislative outcomes favorable to the interests of organized labor. I identify the in-kind contributions in the next section. It is not possible to use accounting methods to measure the dollar value of the unions' in-kind services to the Democratic Party from the unions' published reports, or their financial reports to the Labor Department. But this does not imply that there cannot be an alternative to estimate their dollar value.

The conceptual rationale for seeking an estimate of unions' in-kind contributions is to ask, what would it cost the Democratic Party to purchase the services that unions render to the Party without financial charge? To estimate that value, I apply a ratio between the cash and the in-kind contributions that unions make to the Democratic Party. I identify it as a political ratio; it is a number without units. I gauged the magnitude of the political ratio using information on unions' spending for trade union and all other functions from judicial proceedings in *Communications Workers v. Beck*, 487 U.S. 735 (1988), and *Lehnert v. Ferris Faculty Association*, 643 F, Sup 1306 (1986). In Beck the court concluded that the union, a private sector organization, spent no more than 21 percent of its income on collective bargaining and related purposes. Put another way, the court concluded that the union spent nearly five times as much on purposes other than its trade union functions.

In Lehnert the expenditure on trade union functions was dramatically less. (The Ferris Faculty Association is or was a local affiliate of the Michigan and National Education Associations). The state association, which received most of local members' dues and fees, was found to spend only 3.4 percent of these funds on trade union functions, while the national spent but 2.75 percent of its receipts from the local for such purposes. The exact share of expenditures unions spend on political purposes is not known. However, given that the historic functions of unions were organizing and bargaining and that barely one-fifth was allocated to that purpose in the private sector and less than 5 percent in the public sector, clearly the bulk of union expenditures have been allocated for other purposes, and most likely for political purposes.

Given the often stated intention of the unions' leadership to implement their political objectives, and the range of possibilities opened up by these cases, I judge that a political ratio of cash to in-kind at 3 is reasonable: that for every cash outlay of $1, the value of unions' in-kind contributions to demand political services from the Democratic Party is $3. The amount of income spent, unions' cash contributions were $100 million in 1996. Therefore, the unions' in-kind political contribution had an estimated value of $300 million in the 1996 presidential election cycle. Added to the cash reported, the total value of unions' political contributions for services from the Democratic Party at that time would be $400 million. Since total union cash expenditures are likely to be no less than in other presidential cycle years, the political ratio should be at least the same, if not slightly larger in 2000 and in 2004, as the unions view their situation: twilight for the Old, stagnation for the New Unionism. Finally, the judicial findings in these cases substantiate my claim that there has been a shift of the unions' resource allocation from the trade union to political functions.

Can the Union Movement Sustain $400 Million in Political Expenditures?

My answer is yes. First, in 1995, the union movement was reported (using accounting, not estimation) to have received $12.8 billion in income and to own more than $10 billion in assets. These figures are from the unions' financial reports to the Labor Department (Masters and Atkin 1997, Table 1, 494). However, the figures understate the actual totals because numerous public sector unions are not required to report to the Labor Department under the Labor Management Reporting and Disclosure Act, and would not, therefore, be included in these totals. The two significant omissions are the state and local unions of the National Education Association and the American Federation of Teachers. Data on these two alone would raise the total income of unions by perhaps another $1 billion. The amount by which assets would increase is not known, but it would obviously be substantial.

Another insight into the financial capabilities of unions is the amount of dues income in the unions' treasuries. Using Masters and Atkin's figure of $12.8 billion in 1995, average annual dues per member (all unions) at that time would be $782, or about $65 monthly. Perhaps that included some income from investments and therefore overstates average annual union dues, but offsetting that would be dues not included in their study because, as noted, many wealthy public sector unions were not included in their total of union income. Currently, I estimate that the unions' receipts from dues from 16 million members probably bring in more than $13 billion annually. In addition, there would be income from investments, which are available for general purposes.

What Services Do Unions Demand from the Democratic Party?

Some political services sought by the unions from the Democratic Party are common to both the Old and the New Unionism; others are unique to one or the other branch of the Labor Movement. Most are defensive, or preventive. On the "plus" side, the Labor Movement wants more government expenditures on social programs, medical care, education, minimum wage legislation, and, in general, more government intervention in the economy. Among the common defensive services are restrictions on trade agreements (they seek "fair trade," not free trade), opposition to extending most-favored-nation status to China; new labor laws in both the private and public sectors; defeat of paycheck protection legislation; defeat of vouchers in education. Under the rubric of "fair" trade, the unions' demand that environmental and labor standards be included in trade agreements is actually intended to slow if not halt the importation of certain goods. These demands presume that there are no such standards, or that they are too weak. The International Labor Office (ILO) has promulgated such standards for years, and the U.S. government is a signatory to these agreements. Moreover, as official members of the American delegation to the ILO, union representatives regularly participated in determining these standards. The unions' demand for separate American standards makes them the twenty-first century version of the nineteenth-century Luddites. Adoption of these rules might benefit some organized workers in the private sector, but a far larger group of private sector workers, organized and nonunion (who make up over 90 percent of the private labor market), would lose jobs, especially in the export industries. Needless to say, it will cost all consumers, reduce their standard of living, and reduce the output of the economy. It will adversely affect developing nations struggling to raise living standards and therefore dependent upon markets for their products. The Old Unionism prides itself on efforts to assist low-paid workers in the United States, but it is less sensitive to the needs of the comparably low-paid abroad. The position of the leaders of public sector unions supporting trade restrictions is even less defensible: The output of their members does not enter into the trade accounts, so they have no stake in protectionism. On the contrary, they have a stake in free trade because trade restrictions reduce their members' living standards. Similarly, this applies to the public sector members of private unions—part of a class of unions I have identified as the joint union—who have an internal clash of interests. A particular case in point is the Service Employees International Union, once headed by AFL-CIO president John J. Sweeney. About 75 percent of its members are in the public sector, so their standards of living are damaged by Sweeney's championing of trade restrictions. If the United States has learned anything in the last two decades, it is the value of competition in furnishing goods and services in this, the New Age of Adam Smith.

The low wages paid in many developing countries are always cited as evidence of the exploitation of the workers and the need for strict standards. Perhaps in some instances that is so; in others, the absence of any other employment opportunities in these countries means widespread unemployment and that young women may be forced into prostitution as a means of earning a livelihood. The leadership's demand for across-the-board separate labor and environmental standards is tantamount to obstructionism.

An offshoot of the labor standards argument is periodic admonitions of academics to the Labor Movement to organize abroad with the cooperation of the indigenous union organizations. However, international unionism, while a prized goal of academics and some unionists, has little chance of success. International associations of unions still exist and have accomplished nothing in organizing. Even more to the point, what is to prevent unions in one country from taking advantage of wage and other differentials to cooperate with domestic employers to the disadvantage of their union brethren in another? Such indeed was the case of the Canadian Auto Workers and its former parent organization headquartered in the United States, and noted in Chapter 5.

Immigration is another thorny nettle for the Old Unionism in particular. Historically, the Labor Movement has opposed unrestricted immigration; immigrants were a major source of substitute labor. Efforts to organize them, except historically in the garment trades, failed.

A "bonus" for restrictions on immigration was larger union wage premiums. However, the AFL-CIO adopted a resolution at its October 1999 convention in Los Angeles, which has been called "the capital of immigrant workers" (Bacon 2000, 9), calling for the liberalization of immigration.

An important demand of the Democratic Party's services pursued by the teachers' unions is block opposition to educational vouchers for private schools. The power of the teachers' unions is rooted in their monopoly control of public education; vouchers are a competitive challenge to that monopoly. The Democratic Party's opposition to vouchers assures the teachers' unions of the status quo. So, like their confreres in the private sector, they, too, practice a twenty-first-century version of Luddism. In addition, they push for increased educational expenditures despite the poor performance of a large sector of public education.

Organized labor's partnership with the Democratic Party will lurch further to the Left as the new century unfolds. Because of the future demographics of unionism, as already pointed out, the dominant force within the union movement will become the public sector unions. Atop this group will be the teachers' unions, the NEA and the AFT, and they are much further to the Left than most other unions. As stated before, I expect the two to merge in the near term, creating the largest union in the world. As part of that merger, the NEA will affiliate with the AFL-CIO and, in due course, will supply the leadership of the Federation. That development will further cement the close political relationship between organized labor and the Democratic Party, and their interdependence will inevitably shift the political orientation of both further to the Left.

Should There Be Campaign Finance Limitations on Unions?

In a word, no. My recommendation, which I have consistently held and presented in the past to the congressional and senatorial committees, is that contributions should be unrestricted for labor, business, and individuals, provided there is full and timely disclosure of the identity of the donor, the amounts contributed, and for which campaigns the contributions are made. This includes to individual union members and individual shareholders, and must apply to both cash and in-kind contributions. The most important reason for abandoning regulation of campaign finance is that the regulation will surely fail just as it has in the past. Shrewd attorneys and clever judges have made Swiss cheese of legislation regulating campaign finance. More important, the Supreme Court may strike down the current regulations on campaign finance. There is one legal regulation that emerges from the unions' role in politics that would not likely be subject to judicial challenge—paycheck protection. Paycheck protection legislation would require unions to obtain the signature of members before spending monies for political purposes. The minuscule amount that individual members voluntarily contribute to politics is the strongest argument in favor of the legislation. Parallel legislation is merited for corporate contributions for political purposes. Finally, one may ask, are campaign finance matters the root of the perceived ills of the American political system? Free markets, albeit imperfect, have served this country's economy and society well. Why shouldn't they in the political market? To paraphrase Winston Churchill's comment that "democracy is the worst form of government—except for all the rest," likewise, a free political market would be the worst form of raising contributions— except for all the rest, current and proposed.

The scale of the resources that the unions control and dispense on behalf of the Democrats, financial and in-kind, makes the unions, collectively, the Party's largest investor. If the Democratic Party were a holding company, clearly the dominant shareholder would be the Labor Movement. Although this "ownership" may entitle the unions to rename the Democratic Party as the American Labor Party, that change will not be made because of the historicity and trade value of the Democratic Party's name. Similarly, the leadership of the Democratic Party will continue to remain in the hands of professional Democratic politicians, just as has been the case with the British Labour Party. Because the Democratic Party encompasses numerous and heterogeneous groups (has so many minor "shareholders"), organized labor's power within the Party is enormously enhanced.

In contrast to the solid organizational support for the Democratic Party provided by union leaders, members' support is less enthusiastic financially and in voting: when union members were asked to contribute voluntarily to the unions' political activities, contributions averaged two cents per member! (My calculation from figures of Masters and Jones 1998). Another indicator of the split between members and the institutional leadership were the votes that Bob Dole and George W. Bush received in their presidential campaigns. Dole received the votes of over one-third of union households in 1996, and in 2000 George W. Bush received 37 percent of the votes from union households, as well as 52 percent of the votes of nonunion households (CNN 2000). These results contradict the AFL-CIO's oft-repeated claim that the unions represent and speak for working families:

> WORKING FAMILIES SAY GORE—Although the presidential election remains undecided, working family voters overwhelmingly cast their presidential votes for Al Gore and Joe Lieberman on Election Day. . . . Their 63–32 percent edge for Gore over Gov. George W. Bush helped push the vice president to his lead in the popular vote. (AFL-CIO 2000)

The figures of union members voting for Gore differ from those on union households, reported above, suggesting that some in union households voted for Bush. Among nonunion workers—74 percent of the total population of workers—52 percent voted for Bush and 44 percent for Gore. Because that 8 percentage point difference is of a larger population than the union membership population, it is possible, therefore, that Bush may actually have received the majority of the votes of working families, union and nonunion! Organized labor claims to speak for all working families, but this is a patently false claim given that more than 85 percent of all workers, public and private, do not belong to unions. Nevertheless, the election figures underscore the dependency of the Democratic Party on the unions. In the key battleground states of Michigan, Pennsylvania, and Wisconsin, unions doubtless played a decisive role in winning those states for Gore.

The closeness of the ties of the Labor Movement to the Democratic Party in the 1996 presidential elections was documented in an unpublished Federal Elections Commission report obtained by the press (Drinkard 2000). The FEC reported that the "evidence shows that the AFL-CIO had not merely access to, *but authority to approve or disapprove the DNC's* [Democratic National Committee's] *and the state Democratic committees' plans for political activity in each state*" (Drinkard 2000, emphasis added). The state plans, known as "coordinated campaigns," aided the Democratic party's candidates from the presidency down to the local level. A Democratic National Committee spokeswoman defended the close bonds saying that the party "is proud to work on behalf of working families with our partners in organized labor" (Drinkard 2000). For organized labor, the AFL-CIO's political director said that the coordination between the Democrats and the unions was "nothing new" and that "as long as there have been coordinated campaigns, there has been some type of review process [that is, the right of the unions to veto plans and activities of the Democratic Party], because unions are major contributors to these efforts" (Drinkard 2000). Despite evidence that the unions had veto power over some of the decisions of the DNC, the Federal Election Commission concluded that the ties between organized labor and the Democrats were not illegal. If one were to accept the unions' characterization of its relation to the Democratic Party as a partnership, it is reasonable to conclude that organized labor is the senior partner. Despite its deep involvement in the activities of the Democratic Party, political unionism has not achieved a success equal to the investment. The Republicans still retain control over the House and the Senate, and have won the presidency, a combination of political power not held since 1954. The measure of Republican control is slender, to be sure, but, as in athletic contests, the winner is the winner.

Because of organized labor's political setbacks, legislation that unions have long desired cannot even be contemplated, let alone enacted. The Old Unionism, dating from the Kennedy–Johnson, Carter, and Clinton administrations, sought revisions of the National Labor Relations Act that would enhance its organizational power, but failed in each attempt. The current minority position of the Democratic Party forestalls a current opportunity. The New Unionism, now probably in stagnation, also desires new public policies to enhance its power in numbers and collective bargaining. Two versions of how this might be accomplished have emerged. One is a national labor law encompassing all government employees; the second is transferring all government employees to the jurisdiction of the National Labor Relations Act. Precedents for each approach exist. However, neither is likely in the foreseeable future in light of the Republicans' control of the Congress and the presidency. Even if the Democrats were to regain political power in Washington, their inability to fulfill the goals of the unions, both the Old and New Unionism in the past when they held power, suggests that the legislative route for unions has reached a dead end.

Cyber technology has been proposed as the panacea for the troubled Old Unionism, the expansion of the New Unionism, and to promote the political power of the Labor Movement. Of these, only the political use of cyberspace can have a marked impact. In furtherance of its organizing and political objectives, the AFL-CIO created a website on December 1, 2000, workingfamilies.com. The site is intended to provide the millions of union members and retirees access to the Internet; the Federation also offers them computers at low cost. The AFL-CIO's website is intended to link union members to each other, offering discussion forums, chat rooms, and e-mail networks, which will allow workers to communicate with each other regularly and mobilize their workplaces and communities for causes endorsed by the Federation (Wagner 2000). The new service is an extension of the Union Privilege Benefit Programs set up by the Federation during the 1980s.

The Labor Movement has forcefully demonstrated what it can do politically and fiscally at the local level of government. In 1975, organized municipal employees—teachers and other public employees— brought New York City into de facto bankruptcy. Only the intervention of the State of New York and the abridgement of sovereignty avoided a de jure bankruptcy. In Orange County, California, the teachers demonstrated that the transformed union movement could, in fact, bring a school district into legal bankruptcy. While it may be argued that the actions of private unionism could produce similar results, the fact that public entities could go through a financial workout in order to restore solvency was unheard of prior to the arrival of the "Brave New World" of the American Labor Movement (Chapter 4). The case of the City of New York is especially significant because of the unions' role in pushing the City into de facto bankruptcy, the techniques employed to avoid bankruptcy legally, and the curtailment of sovereignty by the substitution of political appointees for democratically elected governance. Interestingly, these events have never, ever, to my knowledge, made it into the texts on labor relations.

The American Labor Movement and the Democratic Party share a pragmatic political philosophy: more government intervention in labor relations, society, and the economy. In contrast, the founding principles of the Labour Party of Britain were ideological: socialism. Paradoxically, these principles had to be shed in favor of pragmatism, and they succeeded in bringing about the landslide electoral victories of the "New Labour" in Britain. Ideological motivations have always been on the periphery of the philosophy of the American Labor Movement and pragmatism one of its core beliefs. Historically, ideologues sought to steer the union movement toward socialism through comprehensive political action, but without success. Nevertheless, unions have always participated in politics in the United States, and became major participants during the years of Franklin Roosevelt. The CIO originated the practice and term *political action committee*, and there is the apocryphal story that Roosevelt, on being asked for a political decision on some matter on one occasion, was reported to have said, "Clear it with Sidney." The reference was to Sidney Hillman, president of the Amalgamated Clothing Workers, affiliated with the CIO, and the key figure in the CIO's Political Action Committee. Those ties eventually matured close to the end of the twentieth century. If I were to set a date for the emergence of the Democratic Party as the Labor Party of the United States, it occurred in 1984, when the AFL-CIO won the Democratic Party's nomination of Walter Mondale for the presidency. In 1992 and thereafter, the number of union delegates to Democratic Conventions, central to the selection of the Party's presidential candidates, coupled with the unions' financial power, played roles so decisive as to warrant my assertion that the Democratic Party is the Labor Party of the United States.

7

CONCLUSIONS

The Old Unionism is in an irreversible decline. A hundred years ago, the density of the Old Unionism was nearly the same as it is at the beginning of the twenty-first century. It has slipped back by virtually one century. Measured by membership, the Old Unionism has been descending into the twilight zone since peaking in 1970 at 17 million, and, measured by market share (density), it has been in decline since 1953, when it peaked at 36 percent (Troy and Sheflin 1985, Appendix A). Some three decades later, by 2002, membership had shrunk to 9.3 million and density to 8.6 percent. The last time membership in the Old Unionism touched the 9 million mark was in 1942, at 9.7 million members, and at that time it was on the upswing. Historically, the last time its market penetration was in the 8 percent range occurred in 1907, at 7.8 percent, and that, too, preceded a period of growth in density (Troy and Sheflin 1985, Appendix A). Although these figures establish the twilight of the Old Unionism, they do not imply its extinction. Unions and collective bargaining will remain factors in several key industries—auto manufacturing, transportation, and construction. Moreover, with a current membership of over 9 million, the Old Unionism enrolls a larger membership than the total membership, private and public combined, of any of the other G-7 countries, except Japan. Total membership in the United States does not exceed any G-7 country. Moreover, it takes in the largest income and owns the most assets of any of the other union movements. These facts are a predicate for its emerging role in the political life of the country, as it increasingly shifts resources and focus from trade union to political functions.

The shift in emphasis is owed to a great extent to the twilight of the Old Unionism and to the rise of the New Unionism. Although the Old Unionism still accounts for more members, before the decade is out, the

New Unionism will likely be the "majority partner" in the American Labor Movement. Given that the New Unionism negotiates and deals with public bodies daily, it is inherently political, emphasizing the growing politicization of the American Labor Movement. I have already addressed in detail my belief that the nature of the Labor Movement's ties to the Democratic Party are extensive. This development is a watershed in the history of the country and the Labor Movement.

The philosophies of the two wings of the Labor Movement differ on key points, but on the role they expect from the Democratic Party and from government, they are in agreement (Troy 2001). Both want more government intervention: the Old Unionism seeks it to revive membership and share of the market; the New Unionism seeks government intervention to overcome the stagnation currently besetting it. To revive membership, the Old Unionism's agenda is a revised National Labor Relations Act, one more favorable to organizing and bargaining. The prospects of success at this time are nil. But, even if it were possible, the experience of all other G-7 countries, and especially Canada, demonstrates that a more pro-union labor law will not reverse the tide in this, the New Age of Adam Smith. The New Unionism's agenda is for a national law covering all public employees—federal, state, and local. Such legislation is constitutionally possible since *Garcia v. San Antonio Metro. Transit Authority*, 469 US 528 (1985), but the probability of enactment of such legislation is also nil. Another route the New Unionism pursues is extension of coverage under the National Labor Relations Act, but that, too, is most unlikely. The reasons are the present and anticipated make-up of the U.S. Congress, and, perhaps even more important, the federal system itself, that is, the opposition of state and local governments to being subjected to a federal law covering labor relations. I noted that the two wings of the American Labor Movement have differences, even though these do not attract public attention. A leading one is attitudes toward free trade. The Old Unionism opposes opening up free trade, and for that matter, so does the New Unionism. However, the difference is that while free trade can adversely affect workers represented by the Old Unionism, such is not the case for those represented by the New Unionism. Opposition of the New Unionism, that is, of its leaders, to free trade translates into higher costs and reduced-quality products for its members as consumers. However, the interests of members are overridden by the theme of the "Solidarity of Labor."

Despite the continuing flow of evidence that markets and economic and technological changes overwhelm the monopoly power bestowed by labor law on unions, proposals continue to emerge to reverse the ebb of the Old Unionism. Recently, in April 2003, the Ray Marshall Center and the LBJ School of Public Affairs sponsored a conference on "The Future of Labor Unions," the focus of which was to explore remedies for the ailing Old Unionism. (The conference did not devote any attention to the New Unionism, presumably because of the general, but mistaken, belief that this branch of the Labor Movement was in "good health," despite the statistical evidence that it has actually been stagnating over the last decade.) Professor Julius Getman presented one of the principal papers, "Another Look at Labor and the Law" (on which I was a commentator), offering another legal approach to reviving the Old Unionism. Its major thrust was to annul the Supreme Court's decision in *NLRB v. Mackay Radio & Telegraph*, 304 US 333 (1938). In that decision, the Court ruled that employers had the right to permanently replace strikers and that they were not required to discharge the replacements. If this ruling were removed, Getman argued, it would renew the power of the strike, strengthening the unions and thereby attracting unorganized workers. Even if that were achievable, it would still fall prey to the New Age of Adam Smith. The Clinton administration attempted to nullify *Mackay* but failed (*Chamber of Commerce of the United States, et al. v. Robert B. Reich, Secretary of Labor*, No. 95–5242. U.S. Circuit Court of Appeals, District of Columbia Circuit. Decided February 2, 1996, 74 Federal Reporter, 3d Series).

Yet another scheme to revive the Old Unionism was proposed by Richard Freeman at this conference. This one, finally accepting that unions cannot recover in the old-fashioned way, by organizing, proposed minority union representation and, apparently influenced by the Blair government's devolution of some parliamentary authority to Scotland and Wales, proposed sharing (devolution was his word) the authority of the National Labor Relations Act with state and local governments. Neither has a future. The expectation behind minority union representation is the old "boring from within" method, the method that the Communist Party had used in the past: union members in the workplace would be a source of intelligence, heightened in these days by cyberspace. As already noted, cyberspace offers no panacea in organizing. Proportional representation was once tried in the evolution of exclusive representation. The Automobile Labor Board, established by Executive Order of the President (Franklin D. Roosevelt), under the chairmanship of Leo

Wolman applied proportional representation to the industry under section 7(a) of the National Industrial Recovery Act (NIRA). It was strongly opposed by organized labor and ended when the NIRA was declared unconstitutional in 1935. In passing, it is noteworthy that even the AFL-CIO representative at the conference regarded the idea of minority representation as unpromising.

Is there a strategy that the Old Unionism can adopt to reverse its slide into the twilight zone? In a word, no. At best, the Old Unionism faces what in military terms is known as a rear guard action, it is on the defensive and can only expect continued descent into the twilight zone. *More than any other sector of the Old Unionism, manufacturing leads the decline of the Old Unionism. If only two statistics can document the twilight of the Old Unionism, the collapse of its membership and of density in manufacturing are those numbers.*

Without a revival in this industrial sector, there cannot be a recovery for the Old Unionism in general; and none is in sight. Moreover, manufacturing continually undergoes changes to which the Old Unionism has yet to demonstrate its ability to respond. Occupationally, these changes are reflected in the transformation of employment from blue to white collar jobs. White collar employees have historically been difficult to organize in the private labor market, so as manufacturing employs an increasing number of white collar employees, organizing becomes more difficult.

Intellectuals have always pushed for unions to become ideological and for their political action, but unions resisted. Now unions have made the switch for pragmatic reasons (Troy 1999a). The consequence is watershed change in American politics: the Democratic Party has become the Labor Party of the United States.

NOTES

Chapter 1. The Flow and Ebb of the Old Unionism

1. I wish to note that the chapter title inverts Leo Wolman's *Ebb and Flow in Trade Unionism* (National Bureau of Economic Research, 1936).

2. Kondratieff (or Kondratiev) cycles are long-wave economic cycles with a period of approximately fifty years. Nikolai Kondratiev was a Russian professor of economics based in Moscow. He published a paper in 1925 which showed that in capitalist economies there was a historical tendency from the time of the Industrial Revolution to follow a regular long cycle of peaks and troughs.

3. In this book, the American Labor Movement includes all unions, irrespective of affiliation with the original AFL, the original CIO, or the AFL-CIO.

4. Based on my work on union membership at the National Bureau of Economic Research (NBER), I can say that these figures are overstated, but I was unable to develop a comprehensive revision of that year and several years before 1933. These figures are essentially the same as Wolman's in *Ebb and Flow in Trade Unionism*.

5. *Commonwealth v. Hunt*, 45 Mass. 4 Metcalf 111 (1842). The Transportation Act of 1920 and the Railway Labor Act of 1926 provided legal protection of the right to organize to railway employees and, under the Amended Railway Labor Act of 1934, to airline employees.

6. For about two years prior to the formal establishment of the Congress, it was known as the Committee for Industrial Organization. It separated from the AFL, with which a number of unions, including Lewis's Mine Workers, had been affiliates.

7. Lewis was not president of the CIO at the time of the expulsions.

8. The source of this conclusion was a personal comment of John T. Dunlop, who had been vice-chairman of the NWLB.

9. No distribution of locals between the Old and New Unionism (private versus public unions) is available. The figure in the text is my estimate of the number of locals of the Old Unionism.

10. *Garcia v. San Antonio Metropolitan Transit Authority*, 469 U.S. 528 (1985).

11. Wisconsin and New York City preceded the federal government's actions, but were not the catalyst for the spate of public policies that created the New Unionism.

Chapter 2. Why Is the Old Unionism in the Twilight Zone?

1. The G-7 countries are the United States, Japan, Germany, the United Kingdom, France, Italy, and Canada.

2. They included public union statistics in their measure, data that should have been excluded. Public unionism grew over the period of their measurement, thus reducing the actual size of the decline in private density that structural change could explain. As I point out below, while structural change undermined membership and density in the private labor market, government policies and increased public employment *spurred* the growth of public employee organization, the New Unionism. Hence, a politically motivated structural change raised membership and density in the public labor market, just the reverse of what occurred in the private labor market.

3. Comparable data for 1973 for Table 2.1 were not available.

4. I regard these developments as a particularization of Schumpeter's theory of Creative Destruction.

5. The small sample size for the government portion requires me to point out that while the level of densities may be affected, the relationship between the government and private densities is undoubtedly correct.

Chapter 3. Will There Be a Turnaround of the Old Unionism?

1. Prime Minister McKenzie King of Canada had earlier in his career served as an advisor to the Rockefeller interests on labor relations. After a ferocious strike at their mining operations in Colorado, King was brought in to improve labor relations. He introduced employee representation that was administered by the company, a form of representation later banned under the NLRA. However, when King became prime minister of Canada he introduced the forerunner of current Canadian labor law, and included the legitimacy of employee representation plans. They have survived to this time, although they are probably independent of employer control.

Chapter 4. The Brave New World of the American Labor Movement

1. Although it is beyond the scope of this chapter, they also pose a challenge to the education of students. See Peter Brimelow, *The Worm in the Apple: How the Teacher Unions Are Destroying American Education* (Harper Collins, 2003).

2. The national income rather than the gross domestic product is the better reference in income distribution as it is distributed to the factors of production. It is derived from the gross domestic product, but some components of the gross domestic product are not distributed to the factors of production.

3. Although collective bargaining by public employee unions appears to be no different than that between private employers and unions, it is, in fact, different. The "employer" in the public domain is not the same as a private employer because the employees' gains are funded from the income of the community through increased taxation.

4. The principal source of the "Philadelphia Story" is the text of an address by then Mayor Edward G. Rendell to the Manhattan Institute in New York City on November 10, 1993.

5. I assume that there is a state and/or perhaps an L.A. County law that recognizes the rights of workers to form, join, and assist labor organizations of their own choice without interference, but if so, it did not come into play in this instance.

Chapter 5. Is the Twilight of the Old Unionism Unique to the United States?

1. The number of unions with headquarters in the United States and functioning in Canada has declined because of the disaffiliation of a number of Canadian unions from their parent organizations in the United States and also from the AFL-CIO. The reasons are, in some instances, nationalism, and in others, like the Canadian Auto Workers, that unions can successfully hedge against the collective bargaining results of their former American international.

Chapter 6. Is the Democratic Party the Labor Party of the United States?

1. Quoted in Turner, Katz, and Hurd (2001, 1).

BIBLIOGRAPHY

AFL-CIO. 1985. *The Changing Situation of Workers and Their Unions*. Washington, D.C.: AFL-CIO.

————. 2000. "In the 'Cliffhanger' Presidential Election, Massive Mobilization and High Turnout by Union Members Made the Difference in Key States." November 8 (www.aflcio.org/mediacenter/prsptm/pr11082000.cfm).

————. 2002. "Americans Are Anxious About Economy, Skeptical of Corporations, New Independent Research Released by AFL-CIO ." August 29 (www.aflcio.org/mediacenter/prsptm/pr0829b2002.cfm).

Ashenfelter, Orley, and John Pencavel. 1969. "American Trade Union Growth: 1900–60." *Quarterly Journal of Economics* 83, no. 3 (August): 434–48.

Associated Press. 2002. "Philadelphia to Privatize 42 Schools." CNN.com. April 18 (www.cnn.com/2002/fyi/teachers.ednews/04/18/philadelphia.schools.ap/).

Bacon, David. 2000. "Immigrant Workers Ask Labor 'Which Side Are You On?'" *WorkingUSA* 3, no. 5 (January–February): 7–18.

Bain, George S., and Farouk Elsheikh. 1975. *Union Growth and the Business Cycle: An Econometric Analysis*. London: Blackwell.

Barnett, George. 1922. "The Present Position of American Trade Unionism." *American Economic Review* 12, no. 1 (March): 44–55.

————. 1933. "American Trade Unionism and Social Insurance." *American Economic Review* 23, no. 1 (March): 1–15.

Bassett, Philip. 1988. "Non-Unionism Doubled in Four Years, Says Study." *Financial Times*, May 3, 11A.

Beaumont, Phil B. 1987. *The Decline of Trade Union Organisation*. London: Croom Helm.

Bell, Daniel. 1953. "The Next American Labor Movement." *Fortune* 47, no. 4 (April): 120–23 ff.

————. 1954. "Discussion." In *Proceedings of the Seventh Annual Meeting—Industrial Relations Research Association*. Madison, Wisc.: Industrial Relations Research Association.

Bernstein, Irving. 1961. "The Growth of American Unions, 1945–1960." *Labor History* 2, no. 2 (Spring): 131–57.

Blanchflower, David G., and Richard Freeman. 1990. "Going Different Ways: Unionism in the US and Other Advanced OECD Countries." Working paper 3342. Cambridge, Mass.: National Bureau of Economic Research.

Bluestone, Barry, and Bennett Harrison. 1982. *The Deindustrialization of America: Plant Closings, Community Abandonment, and the Dismantling of Basic Industry.* New York: Basic Books.

Bronars, Stephen G., and Donald R. Deere. 1989. "Union Organizing Activity and Union Coverage, 1973–1988." Manuscript.

———. 1989a. "Union Membership, Union Organizing Activity, and the Union Wage Differential, 1973–1988." Paper presented at the Southern Economic Association Meeting. November.

Bureau of National Affairs. 1996. "Union Survival Strategies for the Twenty-First Century." A paper prepared for the ABA Labor Law Conference by AFL-CIO General Counsel Jonathan P. Hiatt and Lee W. Jackson, Esq. *Daily Labor Report*, March 6.

———. 2000. "Report of the General Counsel of the NLRB on Selected Cases of Interest." *Daily Labor Report*, December 14.

Burns, Arthur F. 1934. *Production Trends in the U.S. Since 1870.* New York: National Bureau of Economic Research.

Cable News Network (CNN). 2000. "Election 2000 Exit Polls: National." CNN.com. November 7 (www.cnn.com/ELECTION/2000/epolls/US/P000.html).

Canadian Federation of Labour. 1990. *Assessment of General Public and Membership Attitudes Toward Labour Unions, the Canadian Federation of Labour and Related Issues.* Toronto: Canadian Federation of Labour. June.

Cannato, Vincent J. 2001. *The Ungovernable City: John Lindsay and His Struggle to Save New York.* New York: Basic Books.

Carter, Donald D. 1988. "Canadian Labour Relations Under the Charter: Exploring the Implications." *Relations Industrielles* 43, no. 2 (Summer): 305–19.

———. 1989. "Collective Bargaining Legislation in Canada." In *Union–Management Relations in Canada*, 2d ed., ed. John C. Anderson, Morley Gunderson, and Allen Ponak. New York: Addison-Wesley.

Champion, Marc. 2000. "U.K. Hit Hard in Europe's Auto Cutbacks—Pound's Rise, Aging Plants and Looser Labor Laws Make the Closings Easier." *Wall Street Journal*, December 15, A15.

Commerce Clearing House (CCH). 1989. *Canadian Master Labour Guide.* Don Mills, Ontario: CCH.

Crispo, John. 1990. "First Year of Free Trade: Time for Review." *Globe and Mail*, January 2, A7.

Daily Mail. 2000. "White-Collar Workers' Union Takeover." June 27, 15.

Davis, Colin. 1997. *Power at Odds: The 1922 National Railroad Shopmen's Strike.* Urbana: University of Illinois Press.

Dolin, Kenneth R., and Scott Rozmus. 2000. "Labor Law: Regulating Employee E-Mail." *National Law Journal*, July 31.

Douty, Harry M. 1969. "Prospects for White Collar Unionism." *Monthly Labor Review* 92, no. 1 (January): 31–34.

Drinkard, Jim. 2000. "Unions Had Say in Dems' Spending." *USA Today*, September 5, 1A.

Dunlop Commission on the Future of Worker/Management Relations. 1994. *Fact Finding Report.* Washington, D.C.: U.S. Department of Labor. May.

———. 1994a. *Final Report.* Washington, D.C.: U.S. Department of Labor. December (www.ilr.cornell.edu/library/e_archive/gov_reports/dunlop/dunlop.html).

Easterbrook, Frank H. 1996. "Cyberspace and the Law of the Horse." In *The Law of Cyberspace*. Chicago: University of Chicago Legal Forum.

Economic Council of Canada. 1986. *Minding the Public's Business*. EC 22–135/ 1986. Ottawa, Ontario: Canadian Government Publishing Centre.

Edsall, Thomas. B. 2000. "Unions in High-Tech Fight for Their Future." *Washington Post*, October 31, A8.

Estevao, Marcello, and Saul Lach. 2000. "Measuring Temporary Labor Outsourcing in U.S. Manufacturing." Working Paper 7421. Cambridge, Mass.: National Bureau of Economic Research.

Fabricant, Solomon. 1942. *Employment in Manufacturing 1899–1939*. New York: National Bureau of Economic Research.

Farber, Henry S. 1989. "Trends in Worker Demand for Union Representation." *American Economic Review* 79, no. 2 (May): 166–71.

Farber, Henry S., and Alan B. Krueger. 1993. "Union Membership in the United States: The Decline Continues." In *Employee Representation: Alternatives and Future Directions*, ed. Bruce E. Kaufman and Morris M. Kleiner. Madison, Wisc.: Industrial Relations Research Association.

Farber, Henry S., and Bruce Western. 2000. "Round Up the Usual Suspects: The Decline of Unions in the Private Sector, 1973–1988." Working paper 437. Industrial Relations Section, Princeton University. April.

———. 2001. "Accounting for the Decline of Unions in the Private Sector, 1973– 1998." *Journal of Labor Research* 22, no. 3 (Summer): 459–82.

Fitzgerald, Mark. 1998. "Unions Gain Ground at Paper Web Sites." *Editor & Publisher* 131, no. 37 (September 12): 46.

Franklin, Stephen. 2000. "Unions Set Sights on Takeoff After Boeing Success; Despite High-Tech Workers' Big Victory, Organized Labor May Find White-Collar Professionals Are Too Solitary for Solidarity." *Chicago Tribune*, March 22, B1.

Freeman, Richard B. 1986. "Unionism Comes to the Public Sector." *Journal of Economic Literature* 24, no. 1 (March): 41–86.

———. 1988. "Contraction and Expansion: The Divergence of Private and Public Sector Unionism in the United States." *Journal of Economic Perspectives* 2, no. 2 (spring): 63–88.

———. 1998. "Spurts in Union Growth: Defining Moments and Social Processes." In *The Defining Moment: The Great Depression and the American Economy in the Twentieth Century*, ed. Michael Bordo, Claudia Goldin, and Eugene N. White. Chicago: University of Chicago Press.

Freeman, Richard B., and James Medoff. 1984. *What Do Unions Do?* New York: Basic Books.

Freeman, Richard B., and Joel Rogers. 1993. "Who Speaks for Us? Employee Representation in a Nonunion Labor Market." In *Employee Representation: Alternatives and Future Directions*, ed. Bruce E. Kaufman and Morris M. Kleiner. Madison, Wisc.: Industrial Relations Research Association.

———. 1997. "What Do Workers Want? Voice, Representation, and Power in the American Workplace." Paper read at the 50th New York University Annual Conference on Labor, New York, May. Also published in *Employee Representation in the Emerging Workplace: Alternatives/Supplements to Collective Bargaining*, ed. Samuel Estreicher. Boston: Kluwer Law International, 1999.

Friedman, Sheldon. 1989. "Comments on Glenn Perusek's Paper: The Politics of the US-Canadian Split in the UAW." In *Proceedings of the Forty-First Annual Meeting*. Madison, Wisc.: Industrial Relations Research Association.

Fuchs, Victor F. 1968. *The Service Economy*. New York: National Bureau of Economic Research.

Galenson, Walter. 1960. *The CIO Challenge to the AFL*. Cambridge, Mass.:: Harvard University Press.

Gifford, Court. 2001. *Directory of U.S. Labor Organizations, 2001 Edition*. Washington, D.C.: Bureau of National Affairs.

Gilbert, Alorie. 2002. "Unions a Casualty of Dot-com Shakeout." CNET News.com. January 11 (http://news.com.com/2100–1017–808013.html).

Gindin, Susan E. 1999. *Guide to E-Mail and the Internet in the Workplace*. Washington, D.C.: Bureau of National Affairs.

Goldenberg, Shirley B. 1988. "Public-Sector Labor Relations in Canada." In *Public-Sector Bargaining*, ed. Benjamin Aaron, Joyce M. Najita, and James L. Stern. Washington, D.C.: Bureau of National Affairs.

Greenhouse, Steven. 2000. "Renewing a Union in the New Economy." *New York Times*, December 24, C4.

Hackenberg, Robert A. 2000. "Advancing Applied Anthropology: Joe Hill in Cyberspace: Steps Toward Creating 'One Big Union.'" *Human Organization* 59, no. 3 (Fall): 365–69.

Harris, Louis, and Associates, Inc. 1984. *A Study on the Outlook for Trade Union Organizing*. Study no. 843008. November.

Hills, Stephen M. 1985. "The Attitudes of Union and Nonunion Male Workers Toward Union Representation." *Industrial & Labor Relations Review* 38, no. 2 (January): 179–94.

Hirsch, Barry T. 1991. "Union Coverage and Profitability Among U.S. Firms." *Review of Economics and Statistics*, 73, no. 1 (February): 69–77.

———. 1991a. "Labor Unions and Economic Performance of Firms." Kalamazoo, Mich.: Upjohn Institute for Employment Research.

Hirsch, Barry T., and David A. Macpherson. 2001. *Union Membership and Earnings Data Book: Compilation from the Current Population Survey (2001 Edition)*. Washington, D.C.: Bureau of National Affairs.

———. 2000. *Union Membership and Earnings Data Book: Compilation from the Current Population Survey (2000 Edition)*. Washington, D.C.: Bureau of National Affairs.

———. 2002. *Union Membership and Earnings Data Book: Compilation from the Current Population Survey (2002 Edition)*. Washington, D.C.: Bureau of National Affairs.

———. 2003. *Union Membership and Earnings Data Book: Compilation from the Current Population Survey (2003 Edition)*. Washington, D.C.: Bureau of National Affairs.

Hurd, Richard W. 2000. "Professional Employees and Union Democracy: From Control to Chaos." *Journal of Labor Research* 21, no. 1 (Winter): 103–15.

Huxley, Christopher, David Kettler, and James Struthers. 1986. "Is Canada's Experience 'Especially Instructive'?" In *Unions in Transition: Entering the Second Century*, ed. Seymour Martin Lipset. San Francisco: Institute for Contemporary Studies.

Industrial Workers of the World (IWW). Homepage (www.iww.org).
Jameson, Angela A., Roland Watson, and Martin Fletcher. 2001. "Corus to Shed 6,000 Jobs and More May Go." *London Times*, February 2, p. 4M.
Judis, John B. 2001. "John Sweeney in Trouble. Labor's Love Lost." *The New Republic* 224, no. 26 (June 25): 18–22.
Juravich, Tom, and Kate Bronfenbrenner. 1998. "Preparing for the Worst: Organizing and Staying Organized in the Public Sector." In *Organizing to Win*, ed. Kate Bronfenbrenner, Sheldon Friedman, Richard Hurd, Rudolph Oswald, and Ronald Seeber. Ithaca, N.Y.: ILR Press.
Kassalow, Everett M. 1966. "White Collar Unionism in the United States." In *White-Collar Trade Unions: Contemporary Developments in Industrialized Societies*, ed. Adolf F. Sturmthal. Urbana: University of Illinois Press.
Keddy, John. 1988. "Econometric Analysis of American Trade Union Growth: New Evidence." Honors paper, Economics Department, Rutgers University, Newark, N.J. April.
Knight, David M. 2001. "The New Paradigm of Physician Collective Action." LawMemo.Com (http://lawmemo.com/emp/articles/physicians.htm).
Kochan, Thomas, and Anil Verma. 1989. "A Comparative View of the United States and Canadian Industrial Relations: A Strategic Choice Perspective." Paper presented at the 8th World Congress of the International Industrial Relations Association.
Kochan, Thomas, Harry C. Katz, and Robert B. McKersie. 1986. *The Transformation of American Industrial Relations*. New York: Basic Books.
Koeller, Timothy. 1994. "Union Activity and the Decline in American Trade Union Membership." *Journal of Labor Research* 15, no. 1 (Winter): 19–32.
Kumar, Pradeep, and Dennis Ryan. 1988. *Canadian Union Movement in the 1980s: Perspectives from Union Leaders*. Industrial Relations Center Research and Current Issues Series no. 53. Kingston, Ontario: Queens University.
Kutscher, Ronald E., and Valerie A. Personick. 1986. "Deindustrialization and the Shift to Services." *Monthly Labor Review* 109, no. 6 (June): 3–13.
Labor Research Association. 2001. "U.S. Supreme Court Restricts Collective Bargaining Rights of 'Supervisors.'" LRA Online, Labor Law section. June 1 (www.laborresearch.org/section.php/Labor).
LaLonde, Robert J., and Bernard D. Meltzer. 1991. "Hard Times for Unions: Another Look at the Significance of Employer Illegalities." *University of Chicago Law Review* 58, no. 3 (Summer): 952–1014.
LaLonde, Robert J., Gerard Marschke, and Kenneth Troske. 1996. "Using Longitudinal Data on Establishments to Analyze the Effects of Union Organizing Campaigns in the United States." *Annales D'Economie et de Statistique* 41/42 (January–June): 155–85.
Lewis, Diane E. 2000. "On Lexington Green, A Clash of White and Blue: Raytheon Strike Highlights Firm's Growing Need for More High-Tech Engineers, Fewer Plant Employees." *Boston Globe*, September 1, F1.
Lieberman, Myron. 1997. *The Teacher Unions: How the NEA and AFT Sabotage Reform and Hold Students, Parents, Teachers, and Taxpayers Hostage to Bureaucracy*. New York: Free Press.
Lipset, Seymour M. 1990. "Labor and Socialism in Canada and the United States." Larry Sefton Memorial Lecture, Woodsworth College, University of Toronto.

Lipset, Seymour M., and Noah Meltz. 1996. "Comparative Labour Attitudes Survey. Preliminary Survey Data." Manuscript. September 13.

Little, Jane S. 1988. "At Stake in the US–Canada Free Trade Agreement: Modest Gains or a Significant Setback." *New England Economic Review* (May–June): 3–20.

Long, Richard J. 1993. "The Effect of Unionization on Employment Growth of Canadian Companies." *Industrial & Labor Relations Review* 46, no. 4 (July): 691–703.

Masters, Marick F., and Robert S. Atkin. 1997. "The Finances of Major U.S. Unions." *Industrial Relations*, 36, no. 4 (October): 489–506.

Masters, Marick F., and Ray Jones. 1998. "The Hard and Soft Sides of Union Political Money." *Journal of Labor Research* 20, no. 3 (Summer): 297–327.

Medoff, James L. 1977. "The Public's Image of Labor and Labor's Response." Quality of Employment Survey 1–52, Institute for Social Research, University of Michigan.

Meister, Dick. 2000. "ORGANIZE! ORGANIZE! ORGANIZE!" Labor Net (www.labornet.org/viewpoints/meister/organize.htm).

Meltz, Noah M. 1990. "Unionism in Canada, US: On Parallel Treadmills." *Forum for Applied Research and Public Policy* 5, no. 4: 46–52.

National Labor Relations Board. 1999. *Boston Medical Center Corp.*, 330 NLRB 30, November 26 (www.nlrb.gov/bound330.html).

Neumann, George R., and E.R. Rissman. 1984. "Where Have All the Union Members Gone?" *Journal of Labor Research* 2, no. 2 (April): 175–92.

Organized Labor Accountability Project. Falls Church, Va.: National Legal and Policy Center (www.nlpc.org/olap/index.htm).

Penn & Schoen Associates, Inc. 1993. "The President's Commission for the Future of Worker-Management Relations," a national opinion poll conducted for the Employment Policy Foundation, May 8-10. (Summary available at www.epf.org/commentary/polls/1993/pollLaborComm.pdf)

Perl, Peter. 1987. "The Lifeline for Unions: Recruiting." *Washington Post*, September 13, H1.

Perusek, Glenn. 1989. "The U.S. –Canada Split in the United Automobile Workers." In *Proceedings of the Forty-First Annual Meeting*. Madison, Wisc.: Industrial Relations Research Association.

Phelps Brown, Henry. 1990. "The Counter-Revolution of Our Time." *Industrial Relations* 29, no. 1 (January): 1–40.

Ponak, Allen, and Mark Thompson. 1989. "Public Sector Collective Bargaining." In *Union–Management Relations in Canada*, 2d ed., ed. John C. Anderson, Morley Gunderson, and Allen Ponak. New York: Addison-Wesley.

Purdum, Todd S. 1991. "Dinkins Has a 5-Year Plan; Critics Say It Doesn't Add Up." *New York Times*, November 10, D8.

Robfogel, Susan S. 2000. "Electronic Communication and the NLRA: Union Access and Employer Rights." 2000 Mid-Winter Meeting, American Bar Association Committee on Development of the Law Under the National Labor Relations Act (www.bna.com/bnabooks/ababna/nlra/2000/nlrafogel.pdf).

Rose, Joseph B. 1984. "Growth Patterns of Public Sector Unions." In *Conflict or Compromise: The Future of Public Industrial Relations*, ed. Mark Thompson and Gene Swimmer. Halifax, Nova Scotia: Institute for Research on Public Policy.

Rose, Joseph B., and Gary N. Chaisson. 1987. "The State of the Unions Revisited: The United States and Canada." Paper presented at the Annual Meeting of the Canadian Industrial Relations Association.

———. 1996. "Linking Union Density and Union Effectiveness: The North American Experience." *Industrial Relations* 35, no. 1 (January): 78–105.

Royal Bank of Canada. 1990. "Free Trade Agreement: One-Year Retrospective." *Econoscope*, January 13.

———. 1991. "Free Trade Agreement: Second-Year Review." *Econoscope*, Special Issue, February.

Ryan, Richard A. 2002. "Hoffa Breaks Mold, Backs Pro-Labor GOP Candidates." *Detroit News*, May 26 (www.detnews.com/2002/politics/0205/26/a01-499505.htm).

Safire, William. 1997. "The Demo-Labor Party." *New York Times*, November 12, A31.

Schumpeter, Joseph A. 1975. *Capitalism, Socialism and Democracy*. New York: Harper (orig. pub. 1942).

Shalala, Donna, and Carol Bellamy. 1976. "A State Saves a City: The New York Case." *Duke Law Journal* 25, no. 6 (January): 1119–32.

Sheflin, Neil. 1984. "Transition Function Estimation of Structural Shifts in Models of American Trade Union Growth." *Applied Economics* 16, no. 1 (January): 73–80.

Sheflin, Neil, Leo Troy, and Timothy Koeller. 1981. "Structural Stability in Models of Trade Union Growth." *Quarterly Journal of Economics* 96, no. 1 (February): 77–88.

Shostak, Arthur B. 1999. *CyberUnion: Empowering Labor Through Computer Technology*. Armonk, N.Y.: M.E. Sharpe.

Simmons, C. Gordon, and Kenneth P. Swan. 1982. "Selection of the Bargaining Agent." In *Labour Relations Law in the Public Sector: Cases, Materials and Commentary*, ed. C. Gordon Simmons and Kenneth P. Swan. Kingston, Ontario: Industrial Relations Centre, Queen's University.

Slichter, Sumner. 1948. *Trade Unions in a Free Society*. Cambridge, Mass.: Harvard University Press.

Statistics Canada. 2001. "Fact-sheet on Unionization." *Perspectives on Labour and Income*. August (www.statcan.ca/english/indepth/75-001/archive/peixsuti_unioni1.htm).

Troy, Leo. 1955. *Distribution of Union Membership Among the States, 1939 and 1953*. New York: National Bureau of Economic Research.

———. 1965. *Trade Union Membership, 1897–1962*. New York: National Bureau of Economic Research.

———. 1965a. "Trade Union Membership, 1897–1962." *Review of Economics and Statistics* 47, no. 1 (February): 93–113.

———. 1971. "White Collar Organization in the Federal Service." In *White-Collar Workers*, ed. Albert A. Blum. New York: Random House.

———. 1990. "Is the U.S. Unique in the Decline of Private Sector Unionism?" *Journal of Labor Research* 11, no. 2 (Spring): 111–43.

———. 1990a. "Will a More Interventionist NLRA Revive Organized Labor?" *Harvard Journal of Law & Public Policy*. 13, no. 2 (Spring): 583–633.

———. 1992. "Convergence in International Unionism, etc.: The Case of Canada and the USA." *British Journal of Industrial Relations* 30, no. 1 (March): 1–43.

———. 1994. *The New Unionism in the New Society: Public Sector Unions in the Redistributive State*. Fairfax, Va.: George Mason University Press.

———. 1999. *Beyond Unions and Collective Bargaining*. Armonk, N.Y.: M.E. Sharpe.

———. 1999a. "The Philosophies of American and Canadian Unions." In *Advances in Industrial and Labor Relations* 9. San Francisco: JAI Press.

———. 2000. "U.S. and Canadian Industrial Relations, Convergent or Divergent?" *Industrial Relations* 39, no. 4 (October): 695–713.

———. 2000a. Testimony. *Hearings Before the Committee on Rules and Administration, United States Senate, 106th Congress, 2d Session, On Constitutional Issues Impacting Campaign Reform*, April 12: 425–32 (http://rules.senate.gov/hearings/2000/041200troy.htm).

———. 2000b. "Testimony Before the Subcommittee on Oversight of the House Committee on Ways and Means, Hearing on Disclosure of Political Activities of Tax Exempt Organizations." U.S. House of Representatives, 106th Congress, 2d Session, June 20 (waysandmeans.house.gov/legacy.asp?file=legacy/oversite/106cong/6–20–00/6–20troy.htm).

———. 2001. "Twilight for Organized Labor." *Journal of Labor Research* 22, no. 2 (Spring): 245–59.

———. 2003. "Is the Future of Unionism in Cyber Space?" *Journal of Labor Research* 24, no. 2 (Spring): 257–270.

Troy, Leo, and Neil Sheflin. 1985. *Union Sourcebook: Membership, Structure, Finance, Directory*. West Orange, N.J.: Industrial Relations Data and Information Service.

Turner, Lowell, Harry C. Katz, and Richard W. Hurd. 2001. "Revival of the American Labor Movement: Issues, Problems, Prospects." In *Rekindling the Movement: Labor's Quest for Relevance in the Twenty-First Century*, ed. Lowell Turner, Harry C. Katz, and Richard W. Hurd. Ithaca, N.Y.: ILR Press.

U.S. Bureau of Labor Statistics. 1999. "Union Members in 1998." January 25 (ftp://ftp.bls.gov/pub/news.release/History/union2.012599.news).

———. 2001. "Table 3b. Fastest Growing Occupations, 2000–10." Economic and Employment Projections. December 3 (www.bls.gov/news.release/ecopro.t06.htm).

———. 2002. *Employment and Earnings* 49, no. 3 (March): Table B1.

———. 2003. "Union Members Summary." Union Membership (Annual). February 25 (www.bls.gov/news.release/union2.nr0.htm).

———. 2003a. "Table 1. Union Affiliation of Employed Wage and Salary Workers by Selected Characteristics." Union Membership (Annual). February 25 (www.bls.gov/news.release/union2.t01.htm).

Verma, Anil, and Mark E. Thompson. 1989. "Managerial Strategies in Canada and the U.S. in the 1980's." In *Proceedings of the Forty-First Annual Meeting*. Madison, Wisc.: Industrial Relations Research Association.

Villarejo, Don. 1997. "Five Cents for Fairness: The UFW Strawberry Campaign Goes Public." *Rural California Report* 8, no. 1 (Winter) (www.cirsinc.org/rcr/ufw.html).

Wagner, Cynthia G. 2000. "Cyberunions: Organized Labor Goes Online." *The Futurist* 34, no. 1 (January–February): 7.

Wall Street Journal. 2000. Editorial, "Labor Online," August 29, A26.

Weiler, Paul. 1983. "Promises to Keep: Securing Workers' Rights to Self-Organization Under the NLRA." *Harvard Law Review* 96 (June): 1769–827.

———. 1988. "The Representation Gap in the American Workplace." Unpublished paper.

———. 1990. *Governing the Work Place: The Future of Labor and Employment Law.* Cambridge, Mass.: Harvard University Press.

———. 1991. "Hard Times for Unions: Challenging Times for Scholars." *University of Chicago Law Review* 58, no. 3 (Summer): 1015–24.

Weiss, Manfred. 2003. Personal correspondence. May 9.

Wilcox, Gynne A. 2000. "Section 7 Rights of Employees and Union Access to Employees: Cyber Organizing." *Labor Lawyer* 16 (Fall): 253–68.

Wolman, Leo. 1936. *Ebb and Flow in Trade Unionism.* New York: National Bureau of Economic Research.

———. 1936a. *The Growth of American Trade Unions: 1880–1923.* New York: National Bureau of Economic Research.

Wonnacott, Paul. 1990. "The International Economy: The Challenge of Change." Paper presented at the Southern Economic Association Meeting. November.

INDEX

New Unionism *(continued)*
  collective bargaining in, 71–76,
    96–99
  defined, xiii
  demographic characteristics of, 12,
    26, 27
  dominance in G-7 countries, 9–10
  goals of, 154
  growth of, 11, 28, 101
  international comparisons and, 18–19
  legislation and, 13–14
  municipal governance and, 76–88,
    99–100
    New York, 76–79, 151
    Philadelphia, 81–88, 100
    San Jose school district, 80–81
  origin and development of, 91–96,
    105–106
  philosophy of, 65, 66–67
  political activities of. *See* Political
    unionism
  tech workers and, 60
  wage effect of, 72–75
New York City, bankruptcy of, 75,
  76–79, 151
New York State
  Emergency Financial Control Board,
    77, 79
  Municipal Assistance Corporation
    (MAC), 77–78
  unionization in, 10, 11
NLRB v. Mackay Radio & Telegraph,
  155
Nonunion employee representation, 52
Nonunion labor
  corporate behavior and, 21–22
  employee involvement programs and,
    39–40, 50
  failure of inducements, 48–49
  growth of, 10, 16, 21, 37, 44, 63
  neglected by scholars, xiii–xiv
  open door policy and, 40

Nonunion labor *(continued)*
  rejection of unions, 16, 22, 30,
    31–37, 56, 63
  representation gap argument and,
    38–43
  union unemployment effect and, 37,
    47
North American Free Trade Agreement
  (NAFTA), 24, 137
Nurses, unionization of, 104

O

Occupations
  blue-to-white collar shift in, 12,
    20–21
  expansion of professional jobs,
    104–105
  new technology, 56–57, 60
Office and Professional Workers
    International Union, 66, 103
Old Unionism
  AFL-CIO/Cornell conference on,
    46–47, 49–51
  comparative analysis of. *See*
    Canadian unionism; G-7
    countries
  decentralized structure of, 10
  defined, xiii
  demographic characteristics of, 12,
    26
  dominance of organized labor, xiv, 3,
    9–10
  explanation for decline
    deindustrialization, 43–44
    employee opposition, 30, 31–37,
      46–47, 56
    leadership factors, 12–13, 45–46,
      60
    See also Employer opposition to
      unionism; Structural change
      in labor market

ABOUT THE AUTHOR

Leo Troy is professor of economics at Rutgers University–Newark. He has taught at Rutgers for more than forty years. Professor Troy earned his Ph.D. in economics from Columbia University and is a member of Phi Beta Kappa. He has received numerous awards for his scholarship, including two from the National Science Foundation and two Fulbright Visiting Professorships to England. He has published widely in the field of labor. His most recent books are *Beyond Unions and Collective Bargaining* (M.E. Sharpe, 1999) and *The New Unionism in the New Society* (1994).